Sea Kayak Rescue

The Definitive Guide to Modern
Reentry and Recovery Techniques

"From braces to bow rescues, Schumann and Shriner detail everything you need to know about rescuing yourself when things go awry on the water. This book belongs in your rescue pack every bit as much as a PFD, first-aid kit, and paddlefloat."

—Eugene Buchanan, Editor-in-Chief, *Paddler* magazine

"This book brings something new to the arena of sea kayak rescue techniques— the perspective that an ounce of prevention is worth a pound of rescue."

—James Hopkins, Sea Kayak Association

"The authors present coherent, practical advice on dealing with the common mishaps that are bound to occur in sea kayaking as well as advice on the less likely, but more threatening, situations that paddlers should be prepared for."

—Al Staats, President, North American Water Trails, Inc.

Help Us Keep This Guide Up to Date

Every effort has been made by the authors and editors to make this guide as accurate and useful as possible. However, many things can change after a book is published—new products and information become available, regulations change, techniques evolve, and so forth.

We would love to hear from you concerning your experiences with this guide and how you feel it could be improved and kept up to date. While we may not be able to respond to all comments and suggestions, we'll take them to heart and we'll also make certain to share them with the authors. Please send your comments and suggestions to the following address:

The Globe Pequot Press
Reader Response/Editorial Department
P.O. Box 480
Guilford, CT 06437

Or you may e-mail us at:

editorial@globe-pequot.com

Thanks for your input, and happy paddling!

Sea Kayak Rescue

The Definitive Guide to Modern Reentry and Recovery Techniques

Roger Schumann *and* Jan Shriner

The Globe Pequot Press

Guilford, Connecticut

Cover photos: Front cover photo by Zefa Visual Media-Germany; inset photos courtesy of the authors, Roger Schumann and Jan Shriner; back cover photo by Maite B. McLuen.
Cover design: Libby Kingsbury
Text and layout design: Casey Shain
Interior photos: Photos on pages 5 and 19 by Maite B. McLuen; all others courtesy of the authors.

Library of Congress Cataloging-in-Publication Data
Schumann, Roger.
    Sea kayak rescue : the definitive guide to modern reentry and recovery techniques / Roger Schumann and Jan Shriner.—1st ed.
p. cm.
Includes index.
ISBN 0-7627-0745-3
1. Sea kayaking—Safety measures. 2. Rescues. I. Shriner, Jan. II. Title.

GV788.5 .S387 2001
797.1'224'0289—dc 21

2001023112

Manufactured in the United States of America
First Edition/First Printing

Dedication

We dedicate this manual to our instructor colleagues and our students, past and future, from whom we learn so much.

Contents

Foreword xi

Acknowledgments xiii

Introduction xv

▪ Chapter 1. Preparation and Prevention 1
Common Hazards, Safety Guidelines, and Trip Planning

Rescues, Reentries, Recoveries: What's in a Word? 1
Avoiding Trouble: An Ounce of Prevention 2
Common Hazards 2
Safety Guidelines 4
Trip Planning Tips 10

▪ Chapter 2. Safety Gear in Depth 11
Recommended Equipment, Signaling Devices, Float Plans, and Additional Safety Items

Recommended Equipment...11
Signaling Devices..15
Float Plans 17
Additional Safety Items 17

▪ Chapter 3. Bombproof Your Braces...19
Bracing Basics, Advanced Techniques, and Practice Drills

Bracing Basics 20
    J-Lean, Hip Snap, and Head Dink: Step by Step..20
Braces for Beginners and Beyond: Low and High 21
    Low Brace: Step by Step 22
    High Brace: Step by Step..24
Variations on the Theme and Advanced Braces 25
    Running Low Brace 25
    Low Brace Turn 26
    Sweep Brace 26
    Sculling Brace 26
    Greenland Sculling 27
    Hyper Braces and Eskimo Rolls 27
    Forward Slap Stroke 27
Practice Drills for Bombproofing Your Braces 27

■ Chapter 4. Rescue Practice Sessions 29
Wet Exits, Starting Safely, and Rough-Water Practice Tips

Wet Exits: Before You Get In, You've Got to Get Out...29
Getting Rescues Started 31
A Rough-Water Simulator 32
Rough-Water Practice Tips 33

■ Chapter 5. Best Basic Reentries 35
Paddlefloat Self-Rescue, The T Rescue, and Variations on a T Theme

The Paddlefloat Self-Rescue 35
   Paddlefloat Self-Rescue: Step by Step 36
   The Deck Rigging Method of Paddlefloat Self-Rescue 42
   Fancy Flips: Waterless Righting Techniques 42
   Paddlefloat Self-Rescue Practice Tips 44
The T Rescue 45
   T Rescue: Step by Step...45
   T Rescue Practice Tips 49
Variations on a T Theme: Alternate Model Ts and Other Assisted Rescues 52
   TX Rescue 52
   TX Rescue: Step by Step...53
   Rafted (Assisted) T Rescue 54
   Reenter and Pump 55
   British Style (Between Boat) Reentry..58

■ Chapter 6. Expanding Your Repertoire 61
Scramble, Reenter and Roll, Eskimo Bow Rescues, and Eskimo Rolls

Scramble (Cowboy) Reentry 61
   Scramble: Step by Step 62
   Variations on the Scramble 64
   Scramble Practice Tips 64
Reenter and Roll 64
   Reenter and Roll Using a Paddlefloat: Step by Step 65
The Eskimo Bow Rescue 68

Eskimo Bow Rescue: Step by Step 68
Practicing the Eskimo Bow Rescue 70
Eskimo Rolls: The Ultimate Self-Rescue 73
Sweep Roll 74
C to C Roll 76
Roll Practice Tips 77

■ Chapter 7. Rescues for Special Circumstances 79

Tired Paddlers, Incapacitated Paddlers, Flotation Problems,
Loaded Kayaks, Doubles and Sit-on-Tops, Surf and Rough Water

Sling Rescues for Tired Paddlers 80
Paddlefloat with a Sling Rescue 80
Assisted Rescue with a Sling 82
Sling Tips 84
Incapacitated Paddler Rescues: The Scoop and the Hand of God 86
Scoop Rescue 86
Hand of God Rescue 88
My Deck/Your Deck 89
Cleopatra's Needle and Other Flotation Problems 89
Cleopatra's Needle Rescue: Step by Step 90
Variations on Cleopatra's Needle Rescue 91
Rescuing Loaded Sea Kayaks 92
Self-Rescues for Loaded Sea Kayaks 92
Assisted Reentry Techniques for Loaded Sea Kayaks 92
Double Reentries 92
Righting a Double Kayak from the Water 93
Double Self-Rescue Choices 93
Assisted Reentry Techniques for Doubles 96
Rescue Tips for Loaded Double Sea Kayaks 97
Sit-on-Top Kayaks 98
Self-Recovery for a Sit-on-Top 98
Assisted Reentry for Sit-on-Tops 98
Rescues in Surf, Rock Gardens, and Rough Water 98
Surf Rescues 100
Rock Garden Rescues 100
Rough Water 101

■ Chapter 8. Keeping It All Together 103

Towing Skills and Retrieval of Boats and Swimmers

Towing Skills 103
    When to Tow and the Psychology of Towing 104
    When Not to Tow 105
    Basic Towing Technique: Step by Step 105
    Techniques for One-Paddler Towing 107
    Team Towing Techniques for Two or More Paddlers 108
    Towing Incapacitated Paddlers 110
    Towing Safety 111
    Gear for Towing 111
Retrieving Boats and Swimmers 114
    Boat Retrieval Techniques 114
    Retrieving Swimmers 116

■ Chapter 9. Old-School Rescues and Inflatable Safety Devices 119

HI Rescue 119
All In Rescue 120
Inflatable Devices: Back Up, Sponsons, and Sea-Seat 120

Index 125

About the Authors 127

Foreword

When I returned home from college, I had a formal education and a degree, but I didn't have much sense for what life was like beyond the safe confines of college and of the small town I had grown up in. To begin my exploration of the "real world" I rented a room in Seattle. I liked walking around downtown at odd hours, especially at night when the character of the city streets changed so dramatically from the daytime crowds. There was a lot to see: art galleries, street musicians, and pawn shops. While I found downtown fascinating, I often felt vulnerable on these city streets. I was in pretty good shape and bigger than average, but I hadn't the foggiest idea what to do if I had to defend myself.

When you go sea kayaking, you are entering a different kind of environment, which might be as unfamiliar to you as the city was to me. To be sure, some of the hazards you'll encounter, like high winds and large breaking waves, are fairly obvious. Others, like currents and shoals, are less apparent and apt to sneak up on you. With experience you'll learn when and where it is safe to paddle, but to really broaden your margin of safety you'll also need to learn a number of kayaking skills.

To address my feeling of vulnerability in the city, I enrolled in a tae kwon do class. After several weeks of drills and sparring I learned how to block punches and how to strike an opponent with my fists and feet. The class was also a good reality check; I learned what it felt like to take a kick or a punch. The shock of getting tagged confirmed for me that the best policy, in spite of my growing confidence, was to make every effort to avoid putting myself in a position in which I might have to use my martial arts skills.

Training in kayaking recoveries and rescues will make you a more confident and capable paddler. The wide array of rescue techniques that Roger and Jan present in this book are, in a sense, the "martial arts" of sea kayaking. They are the skills that you need to cope with misadventure, and whether or not you ever need to use them, practicing them will similarly serve as a good reality check. When you work on capsizes, Eskimo rolls, wet exits, and reentry techniques, you'll spend a lot of time in the water. You'll find out what it feels like to be hanging upside down underwater— for most people, it takes some getting used to. You'll find out whether or not you are appropriately dressed for kayaking. If you are not, you might discover how cold water stings the skin, immobilizes your fingers, and clouds your thinking. These are lessons about the "real world" that you need to learn in practice before you commit to paddling away from shore.

Even after you've become proficient at recovery and rescue techniques, practicing them occasionally with your cruising gear aboard will serve as a quick shakedown. You'll be able to assess how well your back-up and rescue equipment is secured on deck, whether or not your hatches are watertight, and how well your cargo below deck is secured against shifting. Crawling across the deck for a reentry will give you a chance to see if any of the gear you are wearing will snag on deck fittings or on equipment. Serious sea kayaking accidents are not often the result of a single catastrophic event. More often things go from bad to worse through a chain of minor glitches, many of which you can discover and remedy in the course of practicing rescues.

Practicing capsizes and recoveries in progressively more challenging conditions will give you a better ability to judge paddling conditions. If the wind and waves are up, the question that you should be asking yourself is not whether you are able to paddle in such conditions, but whether or not you can perform effective rescues in those conditions. While you are paddling, after all, you have both hands on the paddle, your sprayskirt in place, and no water sloshing around in the cockpit. However, when you are doing a reentry and bailing out, at least one of your hands is going to be occupied with other tasks like putting a spray skirt back on or pumping water out of the cockpit. Only by practicing rescue techniques in realistic conditions can you make an accurate assessment of your abilities as a kayaker.

As it is in the martial arts, the point of the training is not to acquire these skills so you can put yourself in dangerous circumstances. In martial arts such as tae kwon do, aikido or judo, the "do" translates as "the way." The practice of a martial art is as much about good judgment as it is about self-defense. So it is with the practice of recoveries and rescues on the water. You may paddle for years and never capsize or never have to come to another kayaker's aid, but the techniques in this book are methods you need to know. Through the practice of the rescues and recoveries that Roger and Jan offer here, you will learn how you and your kayak can be more at ease in the marine environment.

—Christopher Cunningham
Editor, *Sea Kayaker* magazine

Acknowledgments

We owe major gratitude to all the friends who patiently stood by us while we worked on this book, tried to run a growing business, and still have some semblance of a social life. We owe dinners to just about everyone we know these days. We'd like to thank Buck Johnson for his numerous protests about calling these reentry techniques "rescues." A big thanks to all of the instructors who have helped us out while we wrote this book: Willie Williams, Frank Lucian, Dean Partlow, Jon Lindsay, Buck Johnson (again), Tom Shores, Michael Wheatley, and Stacy Holden. Special thanks go to Stacy, who helped out both on the water and in the sea of confusion that is our office; we owe her big time for appearing in and helping with the photos as well. Thanks to Dustin Holden, Cyril Walker, Dave Johnson, and Alto Benedicto, all of whom appeared in and helped with the photos. Thanks to Drew Strizik for assisting with the organization and timeliness of the photos; and to Chris Cunningham, editor of *Sea Kayaker* magazine, for writing the foreword and for publishing so much of our work over the years. Thanks to everyone who participated in the real-life rescue stories, and especially thanks that you trusted us enough to be out there with us paddling with the forces.

Introduction

If you spend enough time in a kayak you will, probably sooner rather than later, find yourself upside down "doing a fish count." It's not a question of *if* you will capsize—but *when*. Generally it happens before you've mastered the Eskimo Roll, so a few seconds later you're floating in the water beside an upturned hull, deciding what to do next. This can be a disaster or no big deal. It will depend on sea conditions and how skilled you are at sea kayak rescues, also known as *reentries* for those who prefer the more modern term.

Most of the techniques used for getting capsized paddlers back into their kayaks are fairly modern inventions, developed over the past century. The original sea kayakers, Arctic seal hunters, stayed in their boats after capsize. They relied almost entirely on a wide variety of Eskimo Rolls to right themselves, because their gear was not oriented toward a wet exit. Their kayaks had little flotation, they had no life vests or personal flotation devices (PFDs), they wore no wet suits or dry suits, and they were often sewn into their cockpits, so exiting the kayak was not an option anyway. In the icy Arctic seas that they paddled, to swim was to die. So they became extremely proficient at rolling, developing dozens of different types of rolls to meet almost any capsize situation. Even if they injured an arm or got one tangled in a harpoon line, they had several styles of one-armed rolls to choose from. If they lost a paddle completely, they could roll using their seal-bladder hunting floats, harpoon throwing sticks, or bare hands. They also trained in kayaking techniques from an early age, relying upon their skills for both their livelihoods and their lives. For them it was roll or die, so they had no use for the reentry methods that are commonplace today.

These days most paddlers rely on their boats for recreation not for food. We learn as adults, paddle in warmer waters in boats that float after capsizing and with sprayskirts that are designed to release, and generally consider our-

Doing a fish count: not if—*but* when.

selves "skilled" if we know how to do a single kind of roll. The typical sea kayaker these days swims—comes out of the boat—after a capsize. Those at the beginner level may know one or two basic rescue techniques, and those who haven't learned yet probably recognize the wisdom of knowing how to deal with the eventual capsize. But any modern paddler, at any skill level, can benefit from the original kayak hunters' philosophy that the more ways you have to recover from a capsize, the safer you'll be on the water. Even paddlers with absolutely bombproof rolls may need to assist other paddlers who don't, so they'll appreciate knowing how to help others back into their kayaks, especially those who are injured or have let go of their boats in rough seas.

We were motivated to write this book because there currently isn't one that deals extensively with modern sea kayak rescue techniques. While most sea kayak instructional books have the requisite chapter on rescues, which may cover two or three of the more common techniques, there is no room in such books—while trying to span everything from navigation and weather to gear and camping—for a thorough discussion of rescues. Sea kayakers looking for more comprehensive coverage of rescue techniques in written form had to sort through years of back issues of *Sea Kayaker* and other paddling magazines. We wrote several of those articles, so we began to compile a list.

As instructor trainers for the American Canoe Association, we have been fortunate enough to work with a wide range of instructors from across the country and around the world. We've learned almost as much as we've taught. Before we certify these instructors, they must be fluent with a variety of rescues and their variations. Instructors are often our toughest students. If they have a better way of doing something, they are generally not shy about telling us. By working with them over the years, we've been in a good position to borrow their ideas, refine them, and then try them out on other instructors and our students for further refinement. In this way we've been able to thoroughly evaluate which rescues work well for which conditions and which type of paddler.

We wrote this book to help modern paddlers expand their rescue and reentry repertoires. We emphasize the methods that have worked best for us, after having evolved through hundreds of students and instructors practicing with us in a wide variety of conditions. We've seen what works (and what doesn't) for many different paddlers—not only in flat-water practice sessions but also in large swells, tidal currents, wind chop, and other real-life situations.

Since the quickest and easiest rescues are the ones you don't have to do, we begin the book by discussing some of the ways that experienced paddlers stay out of trouble in the first place. Next we cover our two favorite bread-and-butter techniques, the Paddlefloat Self-Rescue, so you can rescue yourself, and the T Rescue, so you can quickly rescue other paddlers (or have them rescue you). We also cover several common variations on these rescues. With this base of knowledge, we move on to the more advanced techniques, expanding your repertoire with methods that are faster, albeit requiring more skill and practice to perform successfully. Later chapters are intended to round out your skills, covering towing, retrieval of swimmers who've let go of their kayaks, retrieval of boats and gear, ways to deal with unconscious or incapacitated paddlers, and a variety of "old-school" rescues as well as more recently developed gear, among other things.

The two of us have worked and played on the water together for the past eight seasons, experimenting, practicing, and learning from each other, fellow instructors, and our students. Our education is far from over. New techniques and new twists on old techniques float across our bows all the time. Some are more useful than others, but all reflect the spirit of innovation that helped the original kayakers expand their skills. Far from the last word on the subject, we hope this manual will be a starting point—a catalyst for sea kayakers everywhere to expand their knowledge, increase their safety and comfort, and continue to invent new and ever more efficient techniques.

■ Chapter 1
Preparation and Prevention

■ Common Hazards
■ Safety Guidelines
■ Trip Planning

Rescues, Reentries, Recoveries: What's in a Word?

Since there is some discussion among many sea kayakers these days over the terms *rescue*, *reentry*, and *recovery*, we think a brief definition of these terms is in order. For years, *rescue* has been commonly used as a blanket term to describe any form of recovery after a capsize, whether it meant getting back into a kayak after a wet exit—technically a *reentry*—or other forms of recovery, such as the Eskimo Roll or Bow Rescue, in which you remain in the boat. The trend among some forward-thinking kayak lexicographers nowadays is to do away with the term *rescue*. "If you fall down while snow skiing, is it a *rescue* when you get back up?" an instructor friend of ours is fond of asking. "If you fall off your mountain bike or fall down playing basketball, do you need to be *rescued*? Of course not!" For him, capsizing is just part of the sport—no harm, no foul.

The problem he sees with thinking of what happens after a capsize as a *rescue* is that the word connotes panic and being a victim: Being *rescued* is something bad that happens to you. This type of thinking can discourage experimentation and hamper learning, because new paddlers might be afraid of tipping over lest they end up "having to be rescued." A *reentry* or *recovery*, on the other hand, is something you do, or someone can help you do, for yourself. Tipping over is not a bad thing; it suggests you were pushing the envelope and trying new skills, and that's good. Reentry is also a good thing you can do to recover from your capsize.

While we agree wholeheartedly with this sentiment, we thought it might be confusing to many readers and weaken our credibility if we decided to give new names to all the old standard "rescue" techniques. *Paddlefloat Self-Reentry*, *T Reentry* and *Eskimo Bow Recovery* just don't have the same ring. And somehow the title *Sea Kayak Recovery Manual* just didn't seem as catchy (it sounded more like a twelve-step program for 'yakaholics). Besides, this book also does in fact cover several actual *rescue* techniques, such as the Hand of God and some of the swimmer rescues. So with a nod to tradition but an eye to the future, we've clung to some old-school names while adding, we hope, a modern outlook. Mastering the techniques in this book, *no matter what you choose to call them*, can help you become a better, safer paddler.

Avoiding Trouble: An Ounce of Prevention . . .

Knowing how to recover quickly and efficiently after a capsize is a cornerstone of safe kayaking, and it's the focus of this book. But there is much to be said for keeping out of trouble in the first place. "The best rescue," the saying goes, "is the one that never happens." Although we don't agree blindly with this statement—we feel that there's nothing inherently wrong with a capsize if you have the skills to recover from it quickly and safely—sometimes it *is* more prudent to avoid an area of rough water than to try to do a rescue there. So we'd like to discuss ways that experienced paddlers avoid getting in over their heads in "hot" water in the first place.

When paddlers get into trouble, it is rarely due to making just one mistake. Typically they make a string of mistakes. A classic example of this happened a few years ago off Orcas Island in the San Juan Islands of Washington State. Maybe you've heard the story. According to the account in *Sea Kayaker* magazine, two paddlers capsized a double in rough, fifty-degree water near Point Lawrence. When they didn't immediately wet exit, their companion jumped out of his single kayak to help them. With all of them in the water unable to reenter their kayaks, he opened his rear hatch to retrieve his VHF radio, flooding the hatch; his swamped single sank lower into the waves and floated away. He called a Mayday on the radio while the three of them clung desperately to the swamped double. They drifted in the chilly water for nearly an hour. Moments before losing consciousness and minutes from death, all three were spotted by a sharp-eyed young boy in his father's powerboat, and they were *rescued* from the sea by the Coast Guard.

But their lack of reentry skills was only one of many mistakes. Although they were all wearing their PFDs, which along with an incredible dose of luck probably saved their lives, none wore a wet suit or dry suit. The only signaling device that they could use in case of emergency was stowed inappropriately inside a hatch. But even these mistakes all came after the fact, when they were already in the water. The mistakes they made while still on land were the ones that set the whole fiasco in motion. The marine weather report that day issued gale warnings for the strait north of Point Lawrence. Yet instead of staying in the protected waters near their launch site in the lee of the point (or staying ashore), they paddled offshore in the general direction of the point. Apparently they didn't check this weather report or didn't fully appreciate the implications of a gale warning for winds in excess of 30 knots and choppy seas of 1 to 3 feet. They also either failed to check or to understand the local tidal-current log. This tool, common among San Juan Island boaters, clearly predicted the strong flood current that eventually swept them toward the point and out into the open waters of the Strait of Georgia, where gale-force winds were blowing and rough seas capsized them. Once in the water, not having better rough-water reentry training or skills was their final mistake, and it nearly resulted in a tragedy.

◼ Common Hazards

Such basic blunders are all too common in sea kayak accident reports. Fortunately there are several simple precautions you can take that will help you avoid most of them. Before moving on to these precautions, however, we'd like to briefly discuss a few of the more common hazards.

Cold Water: If you capsize in warm water and don't know how to reenter your kayak, you can drift around for hours and hours, waiting to be discovered and rescued. In cold water, however, an unprotected swimmer's window of opportunity may be measured in mere minutes.

Wind: Paddling in wind causes problems, especially when it blows paddlers away from where

Your degree of exposure is an important safety consideration.

they want to go. Offshore winds, for example, can be particularly hazardous: They blow paddlers away from land and farther out to sea. The wind also forms waves, and the resulting rough seas are a common cause of capsizes.

Currents: Tidal currents create problems similar to those caused by the wind. Ebb currents (outgoing currents caused by a falling tide) at the mouths of rivers and bays have been responsible for several kayaking fatalities, sweeping unprepared paddlers from protected waters out into the open ocean. Tidal currents can also cause tide rips, areas of rough and choppy water that commonly capsize kayakers.

Surf: Areas of breaking waves, especially if the waves are smashing into rocks or against cliffs,

are best avoided by those without strong surf-zone skills, helmets, and Eskimo Rolls.

Points of Land: Headlands and other points of land jutting out into the water tend to concentrate the effects of wind, currents, and surf.

Exposure: Degree of exposure is a significant consideration for kayakers. There is a big difference, for example, between being five minutes from shore and 5 miles. It's also important whether that shore is a protected, sandy beach in town or a stretch of 100-foot wave-pounded cliffs in the wilderness.

Boat Traffic: Although getting run over is not common, be aware that large, fast-moving boats may not be able to see a tiny kayaker (aka "speed bump") or to stop or turn in time to avoid one. Also, big boats make big wakes that can capsize small boats.

Local Hazards and Combinations of Hazards: From shoals, submerged pilings, and shipping channels to afternoon thunderstorms and alligators—every place tends to have its own particular dangers. It's best to learn about these from local boaters—*before* you start paddling there. Hazards can also join forces to create new and even more dangerous conditions. When the wind blows against an opposing current, for example, the resulting seas will be steeper and rougher—especially if it happens, say, off an exposed, rocky headland with breaking surf during a thunderstorm in forty-degree water.

Guidelines to Live By

✔ **Dress for immersion and *wear* your PFD.**

✔ **Check weather forecasts and tide predictions before you launch.**

✔ **Use gear appropriate for the conditions and keep safety items accessible.**

✔ **Know your skills and paddle within your limits.**

✔ **Practice rescue skills regularly and expand your repertoire.**

✔ **Don't paddle in water that's rougher than you've practiced rescues in.**

✔ **Keep it simple.**

✔ **Don't become a victim yourself.**

◼ Safety Guidelines

"The sea has no patience for those who are poorly prepared," long-distance paddler Steph Dutton once told us while wearing an expression mixing a wince with a knowing smile. Steph is best known for paddling 1,300 miles from British Columbia to Baja one summer. Although we do not expect you to take on such epic journeys, we offer these guidelines in the hope that you take Steph's words to heart with preparations of your own.

Dress for Immersion and *Wear* Your PFD

By far the greatest threat to sea kayakers' safety, statistically speaking, is cold water. Immersion hypothermia accounts for the majority of paddling fatalities. Technically, there is nothing dangerous about cold water—until you fall into it. Then water even as warm as seventy degrees can begin to sap vital body heat at a rate some twenty-five times faster than air. In fifty-degree water, most people without a wet suit or some other form of thermal protection will lose consciousness within an hour.

A way that savvy paddlers combat hypothermia is by adhering to the adage "Dress for immersion." This means assuming that you might end up in the drink and dressing accordingly: typically by donning a wet suit or dry suit, depending on the water temperature. A good way to find out if your typical paddling duds offer adequate thermal protection is to practice several reentries in them. If you are shivering after only a few practice rescues, you need more layers. Some paddlers are concerned with overheating while paddling if they overdress. With all that cold water around, however, it's always easier to cool down than to warm back up once you've lost body heat. You can splash water on your face and neck, do an Eskimo Roll if you know how (rotary cooling), or grab someone's bow and dunk your head if you don't have a roll.

Another common safety precaution is to carry a spare set of warm clothes in a waterproof dry bag so that anyone who takes a swim or gets chilled from wind and spray can land to pull out the dry clothes. It's said that when it gets wet, "Cotton kills," so choose synthetic fabrics such as fleece or polypro (or wool) for your spare clothing; these will help keep you warm even if they get wet. A windproof shell over this insulating layer helps prevent windchill. Remember, too, that most of your body heat is lost from your head, so a warm fleece or wool cap makes an excellent heat saver, compact and efficient. Sometimes a paddler can continue with a snack, a warm hat, and an extra layer of dry fleece. Other times a bail-out option needs to be exercised by

This kayaker is properly dressed for immersion and is wearing a PFD.

taking any paddlers who have a nasty case of the shivers to a shelter or by creating a warm place for them.

Whether paddling in warm or cold water, you'll be much safer, statistically speaking, when you're wearing a PFD (personal flotation device or life vest). It doesn't do any good strapped to the deck of your kayak, and studies done on drownings and near drownings indicate that the odds are stacked overwhelmingly in favor of boaters who wear their PFDs.

Check the Weather Forecast and Tide Predictions before You Launch

It's been said that "Everybody talks about the weather, but nobody does anything about it." Weather is typically one of a kayaker's primary concerns. Wind, storms, fog, lightning—all can be hazardous to an unwary paddler. Yet there are several things kayakers can do about the weather besides talk about it. Probably the most important thing you can do about the weather is to remember to check it before going paddling. For many

U.S. and Canadian paddlers, a portable weather radio may be one of the best $25 life-insurance bargains you can buy. It broadcasts a continuous National Weather Service report, typically including wind speeds, storm warnings, and often wave heights. Since the report gets updated every few hours, you can check it prior to launching as well as periodically during the day.

Many other countries have some form of marine weather forecast, assuming you speak the local language well enough to understand it. A good way to find out if one exists in the area you plan to paddle is to ask a yachtie (private sailboat owner). Canny sailors are usually tuned in to whatever local weather report is available. The Internet is also an excellent source of prelaunch weather forecasts, but it may not be as convenient for most people to access while paddling as a weather radio (although those with wireless Internet access might disagree). One of our favorite sites for marine weather around the world is Marineweather.com.

Paddling in remote areas beyond the reach of radio weather broadcasts requires more experience and "sea sense": knowledge of local weather patterns, the ability to read subtle signs of changing conditions, and a bit of luck. Experience and sea sense also come in handy even when paddling in areas well covered by weather reports, since these forecasts have been known to be off the mark on occasion.

For a typical landlubber, checking the weather report means determining if the day is expected to be sunny or cloudy and what the high and low temperatures will be. When you're paddling, the aspect of the weather that generally affects you most is the wind, so note both its speed and its direction. It doesn't take a gale to cause problems. Even a moderate breeze can blow a novice paddler off course into rocks or other hazards; slow your progress to a slog if it's in your face; and build choppy, challenging seas and waves. At only 10 knots (12 miles per hour), whitecaps start forming, and these should be considered danger signs to novices. A 15-knot headwind can cut your average paddling speed in half (from 3 or 4 knots to 2 knots or less), and could turn a relaxing two-hour sunset cruise into a four-hour nightmare in the dark. Only the strongest paddlers will make laborious headway against gusts of 20 to 30 knots or more. A wind in your face can be exhausting, especially since you may be unable to stop and rest, lest you be blown backward. But even a wind at your back may not be the boon you hoped for: The stronger the tailwind, the more difficult steering and balancing become.

To gain more experience in wind, practice paddling and rescue skills in protected areas where the wind will blow you back toward shore onto a safe beach if it overpowers you. Then practice paddling into it, turning your kayak, paddling across the wind, and paddling downwind, to learn how strong a wind you feel comfortable in. Of course, practice your reentries as well.

Waves are another challenge the wind throws your way. The stronger the wind and the longer it blows, combined with the greater the fetch (distance of unobstructed water) that it blows across, the bigger the waves will become. For some paddlers, steep, breaking wind waves of only 1 or 2 feet will make staying upright or performing a reentry quite challenging. Waves can also make launching and landing on exposed beaches difficult or dangerous, especially when they're caused by ocean swell—broad, regular waves, formed by winds from distant storms, that tend to be larger and more powerful than locally produced wind waves. Breaking ocean waves tend to upset a kayak faster and more reliably than just about anything we know.

Because of the potential for injury in the surf, we recommend against trying to learn on your own how to launch and land in waves. Get professional instruction and wear a helmet. Start out in small surf. A rule of thumb we use for students in our beginning surf classes is "don't get in over your head"—that is, don't launch from a beach where the waves are over your head when you're seated in your boat. Watch out for rocks and people in the surf, so you don't hurt yourself or others. Kayaks in the surf can be difficult to control and pose a threat to anyone in the water around you. Some of the more crowded beaches in our area restrict kayaks to protect swimmers. Check with the lifeguards or kayak shops for any restrictions in your area, and give other beachgoers plenty of room. For more tips on managing kayaks in the surf, check out the book *Nigel Foster's Surf Kayaking*, or the videos *Surf Kayaking Fundamentals* by John Lull or *In the Surf* by Kent Ford.

Depending on where you are paddling, checking the tides and currents before you launch can be even more important than checking the weather forecast. In some areas the rise and fall of the tides creates currents that are faster than you can paddle. To take advantage of these currents, and to avoid being swept away by them, it's nice to know how to interpret the local tide and current logs (where they exist) or have enough experience to "read" the water (where they don't). Where strong currents create tide rips and other challenging conditions, either you'll need to have the boating and rescue skills to deal with the rough water, or you'll have to develop the sea sense to avoid it.

In addition to currents, tide height can create hazards. A falling tide could leave you stuck in

It's important to carry critical safety gear, like these pumps, and to stow them in an easily accessible place.

a mudflat overnight, or it could expose dangerous rocks in a surf zone. High tide could cover the only safe landing beach for miles with night or a storm (or both) approaching.

Use Gear Appropriate to the Conditions and Stow Safety Items for Accessibility

In addition to your paddling and rescue skills, your gear, too, needs to be able to meet the demands you place on it. We recently read about a paddler who didn't try a Paddlefloat Reentry after a capsize—although he knew how—because he was afraid he might break the flimsy wooden paddle he was using. He nearly died of hypothermia before being washed to shore.

Think about the worst conditions you are likely to encounter and carry the gear that will help you deal with them. Then stow the gear where you can get to it easily during an emergency. It's a good idea to carry a spare set of warm clothes in a hatch, because you'd need to land to put those on. But a hatch is no place for a marine radio, flares, a paddlefloat, or other safety

gear you might need after a capsize. Find a way to carry such items so that they are secure, watertight, and accessible to you, whether you are in your kayak or in the water. For a more thorough discussion of gear, see the following chapter.

Know Your Skills and Paddle within Your Limits

To keep out of trouble, you'll need to have a clear idea not only of your own skills (and be honest with yourself about assessing them) but also of the skills of your paddling partners. It won't make much difference how bombproof your own Eskimo Roll is in rough seas after you've done the third T Rescue in five minutes on a frightened paddling partner who's becoming hypothermic. Many paddlers use the guidelines handed down from mountaineers and backpackers: The group can go only as fast as its slowest member, and only into conditions that are tolerable to the most conservative voice.

Staying within your limits also implies leaving a margin for error when assessing sea conditions and paddling skills. On the other hand, it is difficult to discover your limits until you exceed them. This is possible to do safely, however, by taking a class or paddling with stronger paddlers whom you trust in an area where you can retreat to calmer waters if necessary. See Chapter 4 for tips on setting up safe rough-water practice sessions.

To stay safe, a group's members will also need to stay close enough to each other to be able to offer assistance. This typically means staying at least within each other's sight—and in rough conditions preferably within earshot as well. There is some disagreement among kayakers about how many members constitutes a safe group. Some argue that at least three paddlers are necessary so that if one gets hurt, the other two can go get help. Others contend that four paddlers are needed so one can stay with the injured paddler while the others go for help. The general agreement, however, is that you should never paddle alone.

We feel that much depends on where you are paddling and your skills. You'll definitely have more options with more paddlers around, but it isn't always possible to scare up an army of companions every time you want to go paddling. The more familiar you are with the area you are paddling, the more experience and skills you have, the more likely you will be able to make an informed decision about how many companions you need to stay within your limits.

Practice Rescue Skills Regularly and Expand Your Repertoire

In our minds, well-practiced rescue skills are a key component of kayaking safety. Without regular practice, your reentry skills get rusty in a hurry, so we suggest practicing almost every time you paddle. This is why we finish all our classes (at every level, from first-time beginner to advanced coastal rock garden) with rescue practice sessions. For our more advanced students, doing a reentry is no big deal. They are able to get themselves and their paddling partners back into their boats smoothly and efficiently in a variety of ways and a variety of conditions. We recommend practicing until you are able to complete the basic reentries in less than a minute or two. Then start learning as many of the more advanced techniques as you can. The more options you have,

It's always safer to paddle in a group. Here's a rescue practice session under the Golden Gate Bridge.

Practice a variety of reentry techniques routinely. This Assisted T Rescue works with doubles and singles.

the safer you'll be. This type of proficiency will build confidence as well as a more realistic understanding of your limits.

Don't Paddle in Water That's Rougher than You've Practiced Rescues In

Following this simple guideline could keep you out of almost any problem. If you capsize, you'll have the confidence to know that you've dealt with similar conditions before. We admit that some "cart before the horse" is suggested here. How are you supposed to practice rescues in rough water if you aren't supposed to paddle there until you've already done so? For rescue practice sessions in rough water, we offer many safety-net precautions in Chapter 4. With some good skills practice under your belt, you can then use this guideline as a tool to help you assess conditions more accurately and avoid getting yourself in over your head.

Keep It Simple

Especially in cold water, where hypothermia is your biggest enemy, whatever gets you out of the sea and back in your boat the quickest gets our vote for a better rescue. Why take the time to swim two kayaks together for an All In Rescue, for example, if a couple of quick Paddlefloat Self-Rescues will do? And during a Paddlefloat Rescue, why take the time to secure your paddle beneath the back-deck bungees if you can learn ways to simply hold it in your hands? We're not saying that gear- and labor-intensive rescues don't have their place, but we prefer techniques that keep your reentry simple and expeditious.

Don't Become a Victim

Your first rule in any rescue situation, as recommended by public-safety professionals from urban firefighters to the Coast Guard, is to avoid becoming a victim yourself. Take a few moments to assess the situation before you go charging into, say, a surf zone or a sea cave only to get hammered like your paddling buddy just did. Don't make a bad situation worse by adding yourself into the "needs help" side of the equation. Sometimes the best thing to do is sit tight, assess the scene, and then choose your best course of action based on the situation.

◼ Trip Planning Tips

So you've practiced your skills, gotten your gear together, dressed appropriately, and checked the weather and tides. Now what? All the preparation in the world can't guarantee your safety. Certain risks are always lurking, which is what keeps the sport interesting for some of us. But there is much you can do to hedge your bets and keep those risks within reason. With experience, you will begin to develop sea sense—the ability to anticipate problems and avoid them.

A key safety concept is to leave a margin for error, no matter what your degree of skill and whatever level of challenge you decide to tackle. (An advanced paddler's play spot might look like a wet coffin to someone else.) Avoid planning trips that you know from the start will be at the outer limits of your abilities. This will give you some cushion if you misjudge the conditions or if they change for the worse.

Having backup plans or bail-outs is another way to stay within your limits. A common strategy for this on day trips is to plan to head from a protected area into more exposed waters by heading *into* the prevailing winds and currents. The idea is that if you start to encounter overly challenging conditions, you can easily retreat downwind back into safer seas. Another common wind-avoiding trick is to paddle early in the morning in areas that tend to have stronger winds in the afternoon. On longer trips where you want to take better advantage of wind and currents by paddling with them, check your chart for good bail-out beaches that you can use if your original plan starts falling apart. Also, don't take weather or tide predictions as gospel. They are only predictions, after all. Learn to rely on your eyes and experience to alert you to unexpected changes.

In general you want to give yourself as many options as possible and avoid making decisions that decrease those options. If you end up in the water, for instance, are you familiar with a variety of recovery options? If you get stranded on a bail-out beach, are you prepared to spend the night? A common denominator in accident reports is paddlers who decided to push on into deteriorating sea conditions rather than going ashore. If you have extra food, water, and shelter so you'll be comfortable, you'll be more likely to make a conservative decision to wait out bad weather.

We use a similar strategy when planning our expeditions in Baja every winter. If we're setting up a ten-day trip with a group we think could comfortably cover 10 miles per day, we don't plan a 100-mile route. That's asking for trouble. Instead we increase our options by scheduling weather days into our itinerary and by bringing a few extra days' food and water. On many occasions we have been forced to use these weather days. But rather than feeling stranded in the desert, running low on water, and wondering how to make up the lost miles, we are able to enjoy a relaxing day off from paddling or some exciting rough-water rescue practice.

Depending where you are paddling, even taxi fare, phone money, or a cell phone could be considered safety gear. Jan was once stranded with her class by high winds on Angel Island in San Francisco Bay. With barely a mile separating them from the mainland shore, it was tempting to attempt a crossing. But the 45-knot gusts and group of relatively inexperienced paddlers suggested otherwise. As it turned out, she'd increased her options by caching some cash in her emergency gear. Instead of braving the breeze, they caught a ferry off the island and a bus back to their cars.

Wherever you plan to paddle, think about all the "what-ifs" and plan accordingly. Leave yourself a margin for error, and be creative. The most important safety skill to develop is your sea sense, and your best piece of safety gear is your brain.

■ Chapter 2
Safety Gear in Depth

- ■ Recommended Equipment
- ■ Signaling Devices
- ■ Float Plans
- ■ Additional Safety Items

Our intention in this chapter is not to cover all kayaking equipment, but rather to describe those items we define as safety gear, with a bias toward what we find works well for us. Whatever safety gear you carry—paddlefloat, radio, flares, sling, and so on—make sure that it is accessible to you when you are in your kayak or in the water, that it will stay secure in the flush of dynamic waters, and that it will stay dry if necessary. A marine radio in a hatch, for example, will stay dry, but it will only serve you if you can land. So we're presenting suggestions here for both the type of gear to use *and* where to stow it.

■ Recommended Equipment

Here's a detailed list of safety gear that we highly recommend. In other words, don't leave home without it.

Tale of Two Swamped Kayaks: one with adequate flotation, one without. Which one would you rather try to reenter in open water?

Kayak with Adequate Flotation

Whether you are paddling a more traditional closed-cockpit–style kayak or an open-cockpit sit-on-top, it needs to have plenty of buoyancy to stay afloat after a capsize. We prefer to paddle closed-cockpit sea touring kayaks with bulkheads fore and aft. If your kayak doesn't have bulkheads, you'll need to add float bags that give it enough flotation for a deep-water reentry. (Note that some paddlers advocate the use of float bags even with bulkheads for extra safety.) A wide variety of so-called recreational kayaks, or rec boats, have gained popularity in recent years because they are wide, stable, and very user friendly. Unfortunately some of them have such oversized cockpits that they become bathtubs when swamped with water after a capsize. Even with float bags, certain styles of rec boats—we refer to these as "wreck boats"—take on so much

Prepared for possible immersion in the 50-degree local waters, the paddler in front is wearing a wetsuit, paddling jacket, and PFD, and she has a paddlefloat, bilge pump, boat with adequate flotation, spray skirt, spare paddle, and other safety gear. The paddler in back—wearing cotton while paddling a "wreck" boat and carrying no safety gear—is a poster child for hypothermia.

water that it is virtually impossible to do any kind of deep-water reentry, solo or assisted. The only way to get the water out of such boats is to wade them to shore. This makes them inherently unseaworthy and unsafe except for pond paddling near shore in shallow water. There are many gradations between touring kayaks and rec boats these days, however, with varying degrees of seaworthiness. The only way to find out for sure whether your rec boat is a potential "wreck boat" is to practice your rescues near shore and see if the boat floats well enough for you to reenter it. A word of caution about float bags: We have seen them come bobbing up out of the bow and float away during rescue practice, so make sure to secure them inside the hull.

A Sturdy Paddle— and a Spare

Choose a paddle that is strong enough to stand up to whatever rough-water paddling and rescues you do without breaking. Then bring along a sturdy spare in case your primary paddle does break

or in case you lose it. Roger likes to carry his spare take-apart on his back deck securely wrapped underneath the bungees so a wave can't wash it away. If he loses his primary paddle in a capsize, he is able to reach back and grab the spare for an Eskimo Roll.

PFD

The Coast Guard requires that each paddler *carry* a Class III PFD (personal flotation device) on the kayak. We recommend PFDs with a short waist and large, roomy armholes because they're more comfortable, so you'll be more likely to actually *wear* yours!

A Sprayskirt to Match Conditions

A loose nylon sprayskirt may not be adequate for some conditions. For rough water, we prefer tight neoprene decks, which don't implode in breaking waves or come off if we have to do an Eskimo Roll.

Thermal Protection

As discussed in Chapter 1, wet suits or dry suits are part of the standard dress code for cold-water paddlers. In our area the typical water temperatures generally range from fifty to sixty degrees year-round, and most local paddlers wear 3-millimeter. farmer john wet suits (long legs, no arms) over a fleece or midweight polypro shirt, covered by a long-sleeved paddling jacket.

Helmet

We recommend wearing a helmet anytime you are in waves or around rocks in rough water. We also use them during rough-water rescue practice, when boats are bouncing around in choppy seas. Use helmets designed for kayaking. We've found that bike helmets and in-line skating helmets don't stand up to a marine environment.

Paddlefloats

All paddlefloats are *not* created equal. Certain features in a paddlefloat can make your reentry more reliable. You are less likely to kick one off the blade during the reentry, for example, if it can be secured to the paddle with a sturdy plastic buckle or pinch lock. Retrofit or avoid both those that rely on air pressure alone and those that use metal hardware or Velcro-type securing, both of which tend to work poorly over time with the wear and tear caused by sand and marine salts.

Higher-volume paddlefloats will provide better flotation, and we highly recommend dual-chambered models: Even if you don't usually need to inflate both sides, it's a big relief to have a backup option if one side fails. Look for large valves to cut down on the huffing and puffing you have to do to inflate them while in the water. Designs made of closed-cell foam are popular in cold-water areas (less than fifty degrees or so), because they're slightly faster to deploy—they don't have to be inflated. However, they are more bulky to stow than a deflated paddlefloat, and they offer less flotation than a high-volume inflatable.

Some gear manufacturers are creating paddlefloats that also function as inflatable backrests or foam seat pads. Forget the dual-purpose idea. A paddlefloat needs to be several times larger than a seat section to function as buoyancy in an emergency. Inflatable back supports are a great idea—just don't expect one to save you from anything but a stiff back. Don't scrimp when it comes to personal safety.

Store your paddlefloat in a place that's easy to reach when you're out of your kayak. Some paddlers like to carry theirs under the deck bungees. We carry ours attached behind our seat to keep our decks clear of gear that can wash loose when launching or landing through surf. We use paddlefloats that can be bungeed in behind the seat, which is an easy area to reach after a capsize, and we leave them attached in use, because the bungee stretches when the paddle goes into position. Some instructors don't like the idea of leashes, because students can become tangled in them. Our feeling is that this is definitely a risk, but it is a lesser evil than losing an unattached float to the wind or sea. Wherever you choose to stow it, make sure to attach the float somehow, so the dynamic forces of water—whether waves, wind chop, or capsize—don't sweep it away.

Bailing Options—Pumps, Sponges, and Bucket

We have had good luck with the simple red-and-gray plastic, handheld bilge pumps that are commonly used for kayaking. They are inexpensive and quite versatile, since they can easily be used to help pump out your partner's kayak as well as your own. Some kayakers swear by foot pumps, and these do offer the advantage that you can have your hands free while pumping, whereas the gray and red pumps require one or both bands to operate. Their main disadvantage in our eyes is that they need to be customized to fit a certain kayak and can't be used to pump out a partner's boat. Electric pumps are also a cool idea, but again, they are a custom item, and in addition to being comparatively expensive, their batteries can fail. A foot or electric pump backed up by a standard hand pump, however, might be the best of both worlds if you're looking for belt-and-suspenders redundancy.

We like to store our pumps under our front-deck bungees for easy access. Some kayakers store their pumps under special bungees fitted below deck, between their knees, to keep their decks clear. Although we, too, prefer to keep most gear off deck, we don't like the idea of having to pop our skirts in rough seas to get out our pumps if we need to pump our partner's boat. Some like to secure their pumps on deck using a line, or lanyard in mariner parlance. Instead of attaching a lanyard to keep our pumps from washing off the deck in surf or heavy seas, we use a surf wrap—winding the bungee once or twice around the handle for extra security while avoiding the possibility of getting tangled in the lanyard. We face the handle end toward us, rather than toward the bow, so it can be reached more easily to unwrap it from the cockpit. We also advise against keeping your pump on the back deck, in your hatches, or in the trunk of your car for the same reason. It will be hard to get to if you need it while sitting in your cockpit.

Although not a crucial safety item, sponges are nice for mopping out of your cockpit the last little bit of water that your pump leaves, but don't expect a sponge to replace a bilge pump in a rescue situation. You just won't be able to move the same volume of water as quickly. Bailers, too, make poor pump substitutes—unless you have a wide-open, canoelike cockpit, there isn't much room in most kayaks to get a bucket (or even a sawed-off bleach bottle, which we've seen some paddlers carry) between your knees to scoop out water.

Rescue Sling or Stirrup

Commonly referred to as a sling or a stirrup, a length of webbing or line tied into a loop can help get a tired swimmer (whether it's a paddling partner or yourself) back into a kayak. We stow ours in a PFD pocket for quick access. For information on how to make a sling, see the section on sling rescues in Chapter 7.

Tow Lines

We recommend one or more per group. Both of us feel naked paddling without our tow belts secured around our waists. Appropriate lengths and types are discussed in Chapter 8.

Sea Socks

For boats without bulkheads, some paddlers use a device called a sea sock. A sea sock is sort of like a giant, baggy, nylon cockpit condom that you sit inside after attaching its rim to your cockpit coaming. The idea is that when you capsize, only the sea sock fills with water; no water enters the bow or stern. A bulkheadless kayak with a sea sock can be T Rescued just like a boat with bulkheads.

Sea socks should always be backed up with float bags in the unlikely event that the rim of the sock gets pulled off with the sprayskirt during a wet exit. For a T Rescue to work smoothly with a loaded kayak with a sea sock, it is important that the gear in the bow is secure. Otherwise it could slide into the cockpit area when the bow is lifted and get in the way of reentry.

We don't especially like sea socks. They are not bad for flat-water touring, but for more advanced conditions we have found them slippery to sit in, reducing our contact with, and our control over, our kayaks during advanced maneuvers such as carving leaned turns, bracing in surf, and Eskimo Rolling. Another potential problem is that the bilge pump can suck in loose fabric from the sock and clog momentarily. Because of these problems, an instructor friend of ours who has years of experience working with a school that regularly uses sea socks refers to them as "sea sucks," and he much prefers boats with bulkheads.

■ Signaling Devices

The two purposes of emergency signaling devices, such as flares, whistles, and radios, are to alert people to your predicament and to help them locate you quickly. We will discuss the devices we find most useful and mention some of the others you might consider.

Depending on where you will be paddling, consider carrying a variety of signaling devices. Many are small enough to carry in multiples, and carrying more than one kind will increase your odds of getting help when you need it. Keep in mind, however, that signaling devices do not inherently guarantee a response—they simply signal your distress. Even if someone sees your alerting flare or hears your Mayday on the radio, they may still need several minutes, several hours, or even several days to mount up the cavalry. So don't wait until your last gasp to call for help. Better yet, take steps to ensure that you don't put yourself into desperate situations in the first place.

Whistles and Air Horns

Small and simple, whistles are one of the more common signaling devices paddlers carry. A little louder and longer lasting than your voice, they are especially good for getting the attention of other kayakers in your group. But their sound may not carry much beyond that. We attach ours to a short lanyard on our PFDs. For a louder blast, some paddlers use compressed-air horn devices, but these are bulkier to carry, and the air canisters can leak over time, rendering them useless. There are also a variety of lung-powered horns and superwhistles available with varying volume-to-bulk ratios.

Mirrors

Another simple and compact device, a signal mirror can be quite effective. Of course, it only works on sunny days for signaling into the sun. We carry ours tethered to the inside of our PFD pockets.

Flares

The Skyblazer pencil flares that kayakers commonly use are relatively inexpensive and easy to carry. Like a skyrocket, these meteor-style flares shoot several hundred feet into the sky and put out a fairly obvious distress signal—assuming, of course, that anyone is around and paying attention to see it. They burn for only about six seconds (about the time it might take for a power boat captain to look down and check her watch) and are not entirely reliable—that is, duds are not uncommon. It's recommended that you carry at least three to compensate for the dud factor, and don't count on the O-rings to keep them dry. We carry ours in a small dry bag on deck or behind the seat. Some paddlers carry them in a PFD pocket using knotted condoms for extra protection.

Flare guns are another option, but they are bulkier and more expensive. We have heard stories of them being used to ward off potentially dangerous intruders such as polar bears in the Arctic; one friend used one to scare off head-hunters in Papua New Guinea. Large parachute flares can be extremely effective, with a burn time of half a minute or more, but they are also quite bulky and expensive. Common handheld auto flares can also be used, but they will probably work better if you are stranded on a beach on land than if you are in the water.

Smoke Signals

Best for daytime use, smoke signals burn for about a minute, creating a highly visible orange cloud that stays in the air longer than most flares. Wind, however, can dissipate the cloud. Some are handheld, but we prefer the type about the size of a film canister that can be tossed into the water. We carry ours in the dry bag with our flares.

Marine Radios and Cell Phones

One advantage of a marine radio is that the Coast Guard and most vessel traffic will be monitoring channel 16 for emergency distress Mayday

Here's a VHF marine radio in use on the water.

contact of an unexpected change of plans, such as being overdue if a bowl of soup waylays you at the cafe next to the takeout. One drawback is that a Mayday call may have to be relayed back to the Coast Guard, making it a less direct method of contacting help. Another disadvantage of the cell phone is that it won't broadcast directly to all vessels in the emergency area.

Whether you carry a marine radio or a cell phone, be sure to carry it in some kind of waterproof system; even VHF radios built for submersion should be protected. Marine stores carry clear dry bags that allow you to operate cell phones or VHF radios right through the bag. This is highly recommended: If you need to use the phone, it is protected from water, and the bag will help it float if you drop it.

Flashlights and Strobes

A simple waterproof flashlight will fulfill your Coast Guard requirement of a white light to be shone while paddling in the dark and could be used to signal for help. At night, a strobe light makes a very effective locator beacon for searchers to hone in on, but strobes are illegal to use except for emergencies.

Dye Markers, Bags, Flags, and EPIRBs

If you have put out a Mayday or shot off a flare and are being searched for from the air, a dye marker stains the water with a bright patch of color that helps the pilot locate you. Bright orange plastic bags or streamers that float in the water beside you also make you easier to spot from the air. Or you can put a bag or distress flag on your paddle and wave it to make yourself more visible to other boats. If you are traveling in remote locations and have several hundred dollars to spare, you might consider an Emergency Position Indicating Radiobeacon, better known as an EPIRB. More commonly carried by cruisers than kayakers, these set off a distress signal when activated that is picked up by a network of search-and-rescue satellites virtually anywhere on the globe.

calls. Many handheld VHF radios also pick up weather broadcasts and have other channels for nonemergency information exchange. The best radios for our use have buttons to push rather than knobs for twisting (it is hard to twist through the bags) and are capable of running off either the rechargeable batteries or regular AA batteries. The disadvantage to marine radios is that they have a limited line-of-site range of only a few miles from sea level. This means there must be some boat traffic nearby or your call will fall on deaf ears. We stow ours in a waterproof bag behind the seat.

Cell phones can be useful if you are in an area with good coverage. They can also be handy for nonemergency calls to alert your float-plan

◼ Float Plans

Leave a written description of yourself, your intended route, your car, and your gear with a reliable friend ashore. Your buddy can then alert search-and-rescue teams to look for you should you become overdue. Here is a sample of what a simple float plan for kayakers might look like:

1. Number in group:

2. Number and color of kayaks in group:

3. Automobile: color, make, license:

4. Expected launch, route, and landing sites:

5. Expecting to return by:

6. If not heard from by _____, please notify (agency and phone number):

7. Optional information: (further description of group members, including medical concerns, paddling abilities, signaling devices on the trip, how well they are prepared with shelter, food, and water):

◼ Additional Safety Items

Depending on where you are paddling, several other pieces of gear could come in handy. First-aid kits range from a day tripper's "ouch pouch" with a few Band-Aids and aspirin to a full-on expedition kit with splints, syringes, and scalpels. Some first-aid training is suggested as well: at least basic first aid and CPR for day trips, and a wilderness first-aid or wilderness first-responder course for more remote locations. A boat repair kit with a roll of all-purpose duct tape has saved our act on several occasions. We keep our first-aid and boat repair kits in a dry bag in a hatch (and carry our first-aid knowledge in our heads).

As discussed earlier in Trip Planning Tips, extra food and water are helpful in case you get stranded. Keeping yourself fueled and hydrated also helps your body ward off hypothermia. We both store snack bars in our PFD pockets and keep plenty of drinking water handy. Trip planning items such as chart, map, compass, tide log, Global Positioning System (GPS), and weather radio can come in handy, especially if you are forced to change your originally planned route during a trip and need to find your way to a bailout site. Often most of these items can be stowed in a hatch, assuming you will land to discuss changes in route. But we typically carry a handheld compass in a PFD pocket to find shore in case a sudden fog blows in, and we usually keep a chart on the front deck when paddling in unfamiliar waters.

For real emergencies, a survival kit with waterproof matches, fire starter, and some type of personal shelter such as a space blanket could come in handy. This can be carried in a hatch, but true survivalists recommend it be carried on your person in case you become separated from your kayak. In some areas items such as bearproof containers for your food, water purifiers, rifles, and bug repellent might also be considered standard-issue safety gear.

Chapter 3
Bombproof Your Braces

- Bracing Basics
- Advanced Techniques
- Practice Drills

It's essential to develop your reentry skills, but a good brace is better than the best rescue. Good for beginners to learn, solid bracing skills are a defining characteristic of more advanced kayakers. Even if you're not the type to seek out waves, tide rips, and other rough seas for the "fun" of it, a sudden squall can turn even the best-planned flat-water cruise into either a nice thrill or a nightmare, depending on your ability to brace.

Essentially bracing is little more than slapping a paddle blade flat against the water and using the water's resistance to produce momentary support to catch yourself from tipping over. But liquid water does not offer very solid support, and there are many subtleties involved in good bracing.

A good brace is better than the best rescue.

Of all the ways floating around nowadays to use your paddle as a brace, some are more effective and modern than others. The following techniques are tried-and-true versions of the braces we've learned and refined over the past several years while working both with top instructors from across the country as well as with less experienced students. We've discovered through the years that certain techniques that advanced paddlers have managed to make work just fine are not necessarily the most effective techniques to teach to others, nor to use ourselves. The bracing techniques we use now are somewhat different from the way we originally learned, but we have found them to be more "bomber" than what we had been using.

■ Bracing Basics

Modern, effective bracing technique combines the laws of physics (a paddle blade slapped flat against the surface, for example, offers more support than a blade that is slicing at an angle into the water) and the mechanics of the human body (certain body and arm positions are inherently stronger than others). A basic concept to keep in mind is that no matter how much a brace may look like a way to use your paddle to get your body *back over your boat*, a more effective technique is actually planting your paddle as a way to rock your boat *back under your body*. This is a subtle but important distinction. To improve bracing skills, it is important to first master the fundamentals of the so-called hip snap or hip flick.

Step 1: J–Leans Off the Bow—
Use a bow for support to practice J–leans.

Step by Step

J–Lean, Hip Snap, & Head Dink

Step 1: J–Leans Off the Bow

A good way to practice J–leans is off the bow of another kayak, focusing on technique over muscle. Hand your paddle to your partner and grab his bow, which should be perpendicular to your kayak, for this example on the right-hand side. Practice leaning your kayak as far on edge as possible toward his kayak without actually leaning on his bow. Use balance to hold yourself up by lifting your left knee and bending your torso to the left to put your head back over your center of gravity against your left shoulder in the J–lean (more of a C–lean, actually) familiar to most kayakers.

Eventually edge your kayak even farther and lean all the way over onto your partner's bow, with your right cheek on your hands. Now raise your left knee to roll the left edge of your kayak past vertical and up against your ribs, with the bottom of your hull facing up. You want your body crunched up sideways into a C–shape as much as possible, as if you were trying to touch your left knee to your left ear. You will need a good, snug-fitting sprayskirt for this drill, since the right side of your cockpit will be submerged.

Step 2: C to C Hip Snap

The next step is to snap from a C-shape on your left side to a C on your right by bringing your right knee up and lowering your right ear toward the water. Leave your cheek against your hands and practice rocking the kayak underneath you as far as possible. Try this back and forth several times. Next use the bow to snap yourself back upright.

Here's a tip: Instead of pushing yourself up with your hands, focus on using your body to

Step 2: C to C Hip Snap—
Practice hip snapping the kayak back underneath you while leaving your head down on your hands.

quickly rock (or *hip snap*) your boat back underneath you, dropping your head to your right shoulder (the *head dink*) as you snap your body into a C-position on the right. Once you can do this using only two fingers on your partner's bow, you are ready to move on to the next step, using

your paddle. Using only two fingers prevents you from pushing down on the bow and *muscling* your way up. You may be able to use muscle to force yourself up off a big, buoyant bow, but if you push too hard on a paddle during a brace, it will only sink.

Option: You can also practice hip snaps by bracing with your paddle off of a partner's bow (as shown in the photo), or by inflating your paddle float and bracing off of it.

Braces for Beginners and Beyond: Low and High

The first braces we teach beginners, and the ones we use most often in rough water ourselves, are the Low Brace and the High Brace. A good place to practice at first is on a sandy beach in water less than a foot deep, shallow enough that you can simply push off the bottom if your brace doesn't work, instead of having to do a wet exit.

Our students often ask us which brace is better, or when to use one instead of the other. We've found that novices often prefer the Low Brace at first because they don't need to tip as far to slap the water. This is also a good brace to use when you are toward the finish of your Forward or Sweep Stroke, because your paddle is already closer to the Low Brace position. High Braces are good toward the beginning of your stroke motion or if your boat has already tipped

Option: Bracing off a partner's bow is a good way to practice hip snaps without risking capsize.

beyond forty-five degrees or so. Once you are heeled well over, it can be difficult to push down with a Low Brace, but you can often still reach up and catch yourself on a High Brace. So it is good to get comfortable with both types and to practice until they are reflexive.

Both braces have four elements in common:

1. **The J–lean**—lifting your knee to edge your kayak as you bend your head against your upper shoulder to get your body into the C–shape over your boat;
2. **The slap**—slapping the paddle blade flat against the water to create momentary support off the surface tension (the Low Brace uses the back of the blade while the High Brace uses the face);
3. **The hip snap**—rocking the kayak back underneath you as you raise your lower knee and drop your head toward the water to put your body into a C on the opposite side;
4. **The recovery**—feathering your paddle blade back to the surface, ready for another brace if necessary.

These steps all happen fast, so let's focus on a few keys that will make each of them more effective.

Step by Step

Low Brace

Step 1: Lean

Starting on the right side again, first get the feel of slapping the water with the back of a flat blade. Don't change your grip. To get the back of the blade flat against the water where it will do the most good, it's important to maintain the normal paddling grip on your paddle and change the angle by rotating your knuckles down toward the water. Beginners often change their grip and rotate the paddle shaft in their hand to practice bracing. For a brace to work in real life, however, there is no time to adjust your grip, so get used to rotating

Low Brace: Step 1: Lean—
Edge your boat, hold the paddle horizontally, keep your elbows up, and tip your head against your shoulder.

Step 2: Slap—
Smack the water with a straight downward motion for maximum support, elbows still up over your nearly horizontal paddle.

Step 3: Hip Snap—
Rock the boat back underneath you by snapping your body into a C with your head against your right shoulder.

Step 4: Recovery—
Feather the blade forward out of the water, ready for another brace.

your fist, not the paddle orientation in your hand.

Now rock your boat up on its right edge by lifting your left knee. Counterbalance by putting your left ear against your left shoulder. Lift your paddle slightly, keeping the flat blade out of the water, poised for a brace. It is a common mistake for beginners to dip their blade into the water at an angle as they lean so that it is already submerged when they slap the water; this sinking paddle offers less support.

Step 2: Slap

As you start to tip toward the water, punch your knuckles down, slapping the back of the right blade flat against the surface. Keep your paddle shaft close to your stomach and your elbows up over your paddle, with your forearms vertical. Basic body mechanics makes this a position of greater leverage than that of allowing your hands to wander toward your knees, where you will be slapping down weakly with forearms parallel to the water. Also, brace at ninety degrees to your boat for maximum effect instead of letting your paddle angle back behind you.

Step 3: Hip Snap

Using the momentary support you gain from slapping your paddle, immediately snap your body into a C on the opposite side by driving your right knee up and dropping your head toward the water, right ear against right shoulder.

Here are a few tips to make the hip snap easier. Rather than using your arms to push yourself up off your paddle, plant the blade and use it as a pivot to rock your kayak back underneath you. Also, don't forget the head dink. If you've done any Eskimo Roll training, you're probably familiar with being told to drop your head toward the water. This is also a key element to good bracing. The little extra oomph you get from dropping your head sometimes makes the difference between barely making it up on a marginal brace and falling back into the water.

Step 4: Recovery

Practice leaving your head down on your shoulder throughout the recovery phase, to emphasize the head dink. After you have hip snapped the kayak back underneath yourself, your paddle blade will be buried in the water. Don't lift up on the flat blade after the brace; you may scoop water and pull yourself back over. Recover your paddle instead by using a *feathering* motion—twisting it vertically to slice the top of the blade out of the water and back up into the normal paddling orientation, where you'll be ready to either paddle or initiate another brace. The old-fashioned "beaver slap" brace—where the flat paddle is drawn awkwardly sideways back across your lap on the recovery phase—is considered passé by most modern instructors.

Be sure to wait until you have finished the hip snap *before* you start any feathering motion with the blade. If you feather the blade while still pushing down on it during the hip snap—a common mistake—your paddle will slice toward the bottom, offering no support.

Step by Step

High Brace

Step 1: Lean

The High Brace uses the same basic body mechanics as the Low Brace, but it employs the face of the blade instead of the back; also, the feathered recovery slices out to the rear. As with the Low Brace, edge your boat to the right, left knee up, body bent into the C-position. Again, don't change your grip on the paddle, and keep the shaft horizontal, parallel to the water. This requires an arm position similar to what you would use at a chin-up bar.

One of the most important differences between the High Brace and Low Brace is the need for safe shoulder positioning on the High Brace. A common kayaking injury is a shoulder dislocation caused by extending your hand up and behind you during a rough-water brace. To avoid this, keep your hand in front of your shoulder, with your elbows down and tucked fairly close to your body, and with the paddle shaft held below chin level.

High Brace: Step 1: Lean—
Rock your boat on its edge, keeping your body bent in a C with your head against your shoulder and the paddle held horizontal.

Step 2: Slap—
Keeping the paddle as horizontal as possible, slap the water with a flat blade.

Step 2: Slap

As you tip, catch yourself by slapping the blade flat on the water. Remember to keep your left hand low so the paddle shaft stays nearly horizontal. A common mistake is to raise the offside hand (the left, in this case) so that the paddle spears into the water at a forty-five-degree angle; this offers less support than a good flat slap. *Safety Reminder:* It is important to keep your hand in front of your shoulder during a High Brace and

Step 3: Hip Snap—
Rock the boat back underneath you by snapping
your body into a C and dropping your head
to the right shoulder.

Step 4: Recovery—
Feather the blade backward out of the water,
ready for another brace.

your elbows tucked close to your body. Extending your arm out behind you while bracing puts your shoulder at risk of injury and is a common cause of shoulder dislocation among kayakers.

Step 3: Hip Snap

Raise your right knee, drop your head against your right shoulder, and snap into C on your right. A good, crisp hip snap and head dink are especially important with a High Brace, since you often tip over farther than with a Low Brace.

Step 4: Recovery

Recover the blade by feathering it out slightly to the rear. As with the Low Brace, be sure to wait until you've finished the hip snap, and keep your head down against your shoulder to emphasize the head dink.

▨ Variations on the Theme and Advanced Braces

Once you've mastered these basic concepts and body positions, you can use them in a variety of different and more advanced techniques that will keep you upright in a wide range of conditions.

Running Low Brace:
This involves skimming the back of a flat paddle blade
behind you for support while moving forward.

Running Low Brace

This variation uses the Low Brace arm position to add stability, especially in rough water, when you are in the vulnerable position of turning around to check on conditions or on paddling partners behind you. With good forward momentum, turn your torso and reach back, letting the back of the blade skim the water like an outrigger, nearly parallel to and about a foot off your stern. Lean slightly on this brace to feel the support of the paddle skimming the surface. If you start to tip, you can push down and hip snap as in a normal Low Brace.

Low Brace Turn:
By pushing your paddle forward, a running low brace becomes a low brace turn that can be used for quick turn-arounds.

Sweep Brace:
Skimming the face of the blade back from the bow offers prolonged support.

Low Brace Turn

If whatever you see aft requires you to turn around quickly, the Running Low Brace can be turned into a *Low Brace Turn*, essentially a hybrid of a Low Brace and a Backward Sweep Stroke. Use a good C-position to put your boat well up on edge and lean onto the paddle so it will act as a rudder, spinning you toward the brace. To avoid sinking farther into the water as your speed slows, push gradually forward and out to the side, then finish by bracing yourself back upright. The key to this more difficult maneuver is to *finesse* the turn without pushing on the paddle too hard too soon, which would kill the forward momentum that makes a smooth turnaround possible. If you finish the brace by turning it into a Backward Sweep Stroke toward the bow in one smooth, continuous motion, you will get that much more of a turn out of the maneuver. The face of the blade can also be used for this move (a High Brace Turn), which allows you to get the boat farther on edge for a turn that can be somewhat sharper but generally not as smooth.

Sweep Brace

Instead of slapping straight down with a High Brace, you can get more prolonged support by sweeping the paddle in an arc from your bow out to the side before bracing up. As with an Eskimo Roll, a slight climbing angle—where the blade is angled toward the surface—is necessary during the sweep to keep your paddle from diving.

Sculling Brace

Skilled paddlers gain even more prolonged support by turning the Sweep Brace into a Sculling Brace. At the end of the Sweep Brace, twist the paddle shaft and push the blade back toward the bow (again, use the face of the blade with a slight climbing angle), then reverse it into another Sweep Brace toward the stern. The repetitious back-and-forth motion supports you for as long as you continue sculling. This can come in

Sculling Brace:
Skimming the blade face back and forth provides the most prolonged support.

handy for getting your legs back into the kayak at the end of a Cowboy Scramble Reentry or after the first of two people in a double has reentered the kayak.

The subtle trick to Sculling Braces is to use just the right amount of climbing angle to create support, much like spreading peanut butter onto soft bread without digging into the bread. Some paddlers rely on speed for support, splashing a lot while they scull frantically back and forth as if dancing the twist. But those who have mastered the technique call it a waltz, sculling forward (one-two-three) and back (one-two–three) in wide, slow, smooth arcs. Also, as with any brace, the more horizontal you can keep your paddle shaft, the more support you will get.

Greenland Sculling

Greenland Sculling is an extreme form of Sculling Brace. Lay your body all the way over into the water, floating at the surface and sculling with just your face exposed. Among the more difficult paddling techniques to master, Greenland Sculling is often used as a party trick to show off, but it is nonetheless very useful as a way to refine a *feel* for your blade for bracing and rolling. It can also be used by tired paddlers after a capsize to scull up to the surface to catch their breath before attempting an Eskimo Roll. The extreme body position required is similar to that in the sweep portion of a roll, in which you reach up toward the surface to get the paddle as horizontal as possible.

Hyper Braces and Eskimo Rolls

The better your bracing skills, the farther you will be able tip over and still brace back up. Just shy of an Eskimo Roll, *Hyper Brace* is our name for an extreme High Brace. Tip all the way over and hit the water before hip snapping back up. The fine line between a Hyper Brace and an actual roll can perhaps be drawn at whether or not the head fully submerges. Also, a roll usually begins with a setup and sweep; however, an Eskimo Roll is essentially an Extreme High Brace initiated from a fully capsized position.

Greenland Sculling:
This is an extreme form of Sculling Brace.

Mastering both techniques can build confidence for paddling in rough seas.

Forward Slap Stroke

This combination of a Forward Stroke and a High Brace is one we teach for use in choppy conditions for paddlers at the edge of their comfort zone. Using a short, choppy forward stroke that slaps the water with the face of the blade held at a forty-five-degree angle affords for both some forward motion and some support. Although this is a somewhat awkward and inefficient way to move forward, it is nonetheless more efficient than a capsize. The blade can be adjusted into more or less of a bracing angle in response to sea conditions and your comfort level.

■ Practice Drills for Bombproofing Your Braces

Whatever braces you use, if they are to work when you need them, the action needs to be reflexive. By the time you decide which brace to use and what the proper technique is, you will probably be upside down. To react quickly and effectively, on the other hand, requires practice. The following drills are a good way to beef up reflexive bracing skills. As mentioned before, practicing in shallow water allows you to push yourself without capsizing; just be careful to maintain safe shoulder position when practicing High Braces.

Low Brace/High Brace Combination Drills

Once you are comfortable with the basics and have developed some finesse and timing, try combining Low Braces and High Braces in quick succession on opposite sides. For example, go directly from a Low Brace on the right to a Low Brace on the left, back and forth several times, then switch to High Braces. Eventually work out more complex routines to gain better control. The trick is to follow whatever series you invent without letting your technique get sloppy: Maintain a horizontal shaft angle, crisp hip snap, head dink, and recovery.

Another good technique for developing reflexive bracing skills is to practice flipping your blade quickly from a Low Brace to a High Brace on the same side, again inventing series of moves that develop your ability to make quick transitions from high to low and from side to side. In a more advanced version of this drill, paddlers start with the Low Brace, pushing the angle of the boat lean to the extreme where the Low Brace is not sufficient so that they must switch to the High Brace to catch themselves. Such switching from Low Braces to High Braces is sometimes necessary in real conditions, and the ability to switch is an indication that the High Brace response is quick and reflexive.

Drills for Simulating Rough Water

No matter how much you practice the above drills, you are still in control of tipping the boat. These drills add a real-life component to practice sessions. One of our favorites we call "the virtual ocean." Have someone standing in waist deep water bouncing your boat around from the bow or stern. The idea is not so much to tip you over, just to make you have to use real braces to keep from tipping over. There are several other ways to simulate rough seas. One is to try paddling with a swimmer on your back deck (as described in the Back Deck Swimmer Rescue in the chapter on

Two kayakers practice their bracing while rear deck passengers create simulated rough water.

towing). This helps develop braces in combination with Forward Strokes, and is a good way to practice the Slap Stroke mentioned above. Another way is to paddle a swamped kayak, or try raising your center of gravity with a seat pad or even sitting on your back deck.

Actual Rough Water Practice

Practicing in actual rough water is the best way to gain skills and confidence, provided you can find a place to do so safely with skilled paddlers around to help out. Try paddling in wind chop in a place where the wind is blowing onshore toward a sandy beach with no swimmers, currents, or rocks. Playing in tide rips can also help you work on your braces; just watch out for what is "down stream" the same as you would for practicing in the wind. Getting instruction in the surf zone or on a whitewater river are both excellent ways to learn to use braces reflexively, but getting competent instruction and wearing a helmet are essential.

After developing good bracing skills, many paddlers not only become more comfortable in rough water but even come to enjoy paddling in it. But regardless of whether you go out in search of heavy seas or they come around to find you, good braces are your key to staying upright.

■ Chapter 4
Rescue Practice Sessions

- ■ Wet Exits
- ■ Starting Safely
- ■ Rough-Water Practice Tips

We believe that practicing rescues regularly is extremely important. Whatever kind of water you are paddling in is the kind of water to practice rescues in. This is why we practice rescues in all our classes at every level, from first-time beginner to advanced rock garden and instructor training. At first many beginning students seem reluctant to get wet. But afterward, when they are warm and dry, rescue practice is mentioned time and again as their favorite part of class. We've found that as they progress, our more advanced students start to look forward to practice sessions. The more times they go into the water, the less they seem to fear it. Not only do they find that regular practice builds confidence, but most even start to think of it as fun. No accounting for taste, we guess.

■ Wet Exits: Before You Get In, You've Got to Get Out

The wet exit practice starts on land with a "dry exit": removal of your sprayskirt from the coaming while sitting upright. To simulate being underwater, close your eyes and hold your breath. Locate the cockpit coaming nearest your hips, then slide your hands along each side of it toward the front to the grab loop. (When truly underwater, people tend to reach past the grab loop into the bungees or even to the pump handle if they don't follow the coaming.) Grasping the grab loop, lock your elbows straight and lean forward to release the rand (the tight rubber seal or shock cord) of the sprayskirt from the edge of the coaming. Relax, then find the coaming by your hips under the now-released sprayskirt and prepare to push your hips out of the seat. Sliding your thumbs under the skirt near your hips will help clear the skirt from the coaming behind you. Once you feel comfortable with the moves, try it in the water.

Practice in the water begins with a check that you have enough water depth—usually about waist deep—to capsize without hitting your head. Someone may assist you by standing in the water nearby for your first time, providing some moral support and ensuring your success.

that you have control over it even in rough water.

As you exit the kayak, keep one foot in the cockpit, leaving the boat upside down so the wet exit. Develop the habit of hanging on to both of them during drift away from you in current or wind. Develop (with proper flotation) should float, but they will swimming with your kayak and paddle, which underwater). When your head resurfaces, you are (with the addition of being upside down and is similar to that of pulling off a pair of jeans sensation of removing the kayak from your hips rand, and slide your body out of the kayak. The onds, you will find the grab loop, release the practiced on land beforehand. Within a few sec- Relax and go through the same motions that you through your nostrils to keep the water out. where you will blow a gentle stream of air breath and hold it until you are underwater, Visualize a controlled wet exit. Take a deep

There are three ways to keep track of your paddle throughout the wet exit. One method requires keeping the paddle locked in your domi- nant hand throughout the exit. The second way is to release the paddle just as you contact the grab loop, keeping it in between your inner arm and your chest as you push the rand away from the coaming, then pick it up again as your hands relocate the coaming on your way out. The third method requires a little hardware to leash the paddle to you or your kayak. We prefer the first two methods because they are simple to learn and require no extra gear for you to get tangled in.

It's important to practice the wet exit until you are comfortable with it, but the technique does require an inordinate amount of energy in cold water. In colder locations people often practice their first wet exits in swimming pools.

Waiting to inhale . . .

■ Getting Rescues Started

Some do their first rescue practices in swimming pools; others choose lakes, reservoirs, bays, or sloughs. Wherever you start working on your reentry skills, the water should ideally be very still. If there is any breeze at all, it should blow in the direction of a gentle, obstacle-free shoreline nearby. The water can be quite shallow. We generally start our students on the sand for their first Paddlefloat Self-Rescue, and then move into knee-deep water for more practice on that and the T Rescue. This kind of practice does not allow for a wet exit, so students start by wading their kayaks into the water. The advantage of starting in the shallows in our area is that it reduces the amount of time and energy people spend immersed in cold water, allowing them to focus on learning clean technique. When we then move to practice deep-water rescues for the first time, they experi-

ence greater success, having gained some "muscle memory" from the shallow-water practice.

During your first year of paddling, practice rescues near religiously every time you go out until they became second nature, even boring. Pay close attention to the details, transitions, and balance points. Then work on variations and continue to practice regularly. Practice is the only way to discover which rescues will (or won't) work for you in rough water, and to keep your skills sharp.

Eventually it's important to practice in the type of conditions that are likely to cause a capsize in the first place. You'll discover the many ways rough water has to complicate standard rescues. Everything gets a little harder. Boats, paddles, and rescue floats quickly wash out of reach. If you do manage to hang on to the critical stuff, you may get blown into a surf zone or shipping channel before the rescue is finished, or your

Start your Paddlefloat Rescue practice in the shallows, preferably with coaching from an instructor.

boat might fill with water faster than you can pump. In rough water balancing is tricky and little things do go wrong, just like Murphy said.

A Rough-Water Simulator

Although it makes an excellent training ground, rough water is not always convenient to come by, and the catch-22 is that if it's not safe to paddle in rough water before you've practiced rescues in it, how are you supposed to get rough-water prac- tice in the first place? Before you take your flat- water rescues out into a typhoon, practice them in virtual rough water first. You don't need to find rough water. Just create some of your own.

Take turns playing "Virtual Ocean" with your rescue partner. The partner plays the part of Ocean by standing in waist-deep water, bouncing and twisting the bow of the capsized boat while you attempt to reenter. Then switch roles. The idea at first is for Ocean to make things slightly challenging. Later, as skills improve, let all hell break loose. A variation on this for two-person rescues is for Ocean to stand on the decks of the rafted boats, one foot on each boat, and "make waves" by running in place as if on a Stairmaster, bouncing up and down, or dancing the jitterbug.

When you can get back into your boat despite the worst that Virtual Ocean can throw at you, and you can do it in well under two minutes, you're ready to test yourself in the actual sea. In addition to being effective, a good rough-water reentry is also quick, so you don't end up drifting from bad conditions to worse with hypothermia creeping in to complicate matters. It's good if you can reenter your kayak in less than two minutes; the closer to one minute, the better, and anything under a minute is excellent.

In time you can graduate to the "rough water simulator."

■ Rough-Water Practice Tips

As with real estate, *location* is crucial for rough-water training sessions. When it's windy, make sure to choose a site with onshore winds and a soft, sandy beach to wash into if you don't finish reentering fast enough. (Later you can add challenge by using a buoy or other marker as a pretend reef or surf-pounded cliff that you must complete the rescue before blowing past.) A tide rip makes another handy practice area, assuming it is sweeping you into an eddy and not out into the shipping lanes. A typhoon is not necessary, or even recommended, as a training ground. Start gradually in whatever conditions are "rough" for you; if you regularly paddle flat water, then the foot of chop kicked up by the 15-knot afternoon winds you typically paddle home in would be a good place to start. Ideally you'll have a seasoned instructor or rough-water paddler around to keep an eye on things. The rougher the water you eventually practice in, the more you'll expand your margin of safety, as well as your confidence and your comfort zone. But besides being good for you, rough-water rescue practice can also be fun.

The idea of practicing in rough water is to discover which reentries work best for you in which situations. Each rough-water situation is a little different; a persistent wind will create challenges that rolling swells do not. With practice you'll learn to anticipate problems, and you'll probably develop a few twists and tricks of your own, which is the whole point. Practice to fine-tune your favorite reentries and develop a few backups. You'll be that much safer on the water—especially when you end up *in* it.

Practicing in various rough water conditions will increase your margin of safety and build your confidence.

▣ Chapter 5
Best Basic Reentries

▣ Paddlefloat Self-Rescue

▣ The T Rescue

▣ Variations on a T Theme

There are many rescue techniques to choose from, and we suggest you learn as many as possible. But you have to start somewhere. It's wise to have at least one good form of self-rescue, so you can get yourself back into your kayak, and one good assisted rescue, so you can get your paddling partners back into *their* boats. When it comes to which reentries should be learned first, instructors generally agree that the Paddlefloat Self-Rescue and the T Rescue are the best two for most paddlers to begin with. They are widely considered the most versatile and the easiest to learn. There are quicker recovery techniques, to be sure, but they also tend to be more difficult to learn. When it comes to basic, bread-and-butter backups, we recommend these two techniques as the heart and soul of a modern paddler's rescue quiver.

▣ The Paddlefloat Self-Rescue

These days the Paddlefloat Self-Rescue is widely considered essential for sea kayakers. We'd even go so far as to recommend that no paddler leave shore without it. Even if you'd never consider paddling solo, you can easily find yourself alone in the water if you get separated from your group or if the sudden wave or gust that knocks you in the drink also capsizes your partners. For this reason, we believe that kayakers should be self-sufficient and have a quick, simple, and reliable form of self-rescue. For most sea kayakers, the Paddlefloat Rescue is it. Other more advanced techniques might get you back into the boat faster, but this reentry anchors each of our personal rescue repertoires. And even if your Eskimo Roll is great, it doesn't hurt to have a solid backup rescue.

Basically this reentry gets its name from an inflatable bag or foam block—called a paddlefloat—that slips over one end of the paddle and works as an outrigger to stabilize the kayak, allowing the lone swimmer to climb back aboard. A pump is then used to drain the water from the cockpit. Technique and practice are what make this rescue effective. The amount of practice and the attention to certain details will determine whether this rescue will work only in flat water or in a wide variety of rough-water sea conditions.

Step by Step

Paddlefloat Self-Rescue

Step 1: Secure the Paddlefloat

After calmly wet exiting, the first order of business is remembering to hold on to your kayak and paddle. Because the wind can easily blow your boat away faster than you can swim, get in the habit of using good rough-water technique even when you're practicing in flat water. Hook one or both feet back up into the cockpit to keep the boat next to you; don't bother flipping the kayak right-side up at this point.

With your kayak upside down and your foot in the cockpit, both hands will be free to manipulate the paddlefloat out of its stowage and slide it onto the paddle blade, much the way you'd put a pillowcase on a pillow. Some paddlers advocate righting the kayak and putting your arm through the deck rigging. We don't teach this, because not only will turning the kayak upright raise its profile in the wind so it can blow away faster but you'll also hamper the use of that arm by strapping it into the rigging.

Once they're on the blade, most paddlefloats have a way of attaching securely to the paddle—some type of strap or pinch lock—so they don't get kicked off during the rescue. Secure this attachment and inflate the float (unless, of course, it's a solid–foam type). Don't inflate the paddlefloat until after it's secured onto the paddle, because it will be much harder to slip onto the blade once it's full of air. However, we sometimes carry our paddlefloats partially inflated to speed the process. We prefer large-volume, dual-chambered, inflatable paddlefloats, as described in Chapter 2. Some paddlers need to inflate both chambers to provide enough flotation for an effective reentry. This is a good thing to experiment with before you really need it.

Option: If you are in very cold water, you might try pulling your torso across the stern of

**Paddlefloat Self-Rescue: Step 1:
Secure the Paddlefloat—**
Slide the paddlefloat onto your paddle and inflate it, hooking your foot in the cockpit to keep the kayak from drifting away in the wind.

the overturned kayak, or try straddling it, while you put the paddlefloat onto the paddle, but this balancing act can be difficult. You'll need to be careful not to lose contact with the kayak if you fall off the hull.

Students often ask whether to orient the kayak upwind or downwind from themselves. Although there are those who like the added security of the wind blowing the kayak toward them, others don't like the upwind kayak blowing into their heads while they set up (they might be the ones who don't put a foot into the cockpit). We recommend that you don't worry about where the wind is coming from; just stay focused on the task, with your leg in the cockpit of the overturned kayak. We've found that either side will work just fine in rough water if your technique is good. So if you're immersed and losing body heat, it isn't worth the time and energy spent to switch sides, especially since the sea may spin you around anyway as you try to complete the rescue.

Step 2: Flip the Kayak—
Quickly right the kayak, trying to minimize the amount of water you scoop into the cockpit.

Step 3: Orient the Outrigger and Yourself—
Position yourself in back of the cockpit with the paddle grasped firmly, perpendicular to the kayak.

Step 2: Flip the Kayak

When you are finished blowing up the float, lay the paddle between you and the boat, parallel to the kayak, and grasp the cockpit coaming on either side. If you reach *under* the paddle to grab the far side of the cockpit in one hand and reach *over* the paddle to grab the cockpit on the near side with the other hand, the paddle won't fly up and hit you in the face when you flip the kayak.

Now flip the kayak by pushing the near side vigorously up and away from you as you pull the far side toward you in a quick push-pull snap. The kayak is now right-side up, carrying gallons of water. By flipping the kayak as quickly as possible, you'll minimize the amount of water you scoop into the cockpit. We've seen some paddlers reach across the top of the kayak to right it, but the extra body weight on the boat only increases the amount of water entering the cockpit. There are some techniques—the Bow Lift and the Stern Push—described later in this chapter that greatly reduce the amount of water scooped into the cockpit when the boat is righted.

Step 3: Orient the Outrigger and Yourself
"Back, Back, Back"

Place the paddle shaft across the kayak at a right angle with the paddlefloat resting on the water on your side of the kayak. The shaft of the paddle lies behind the coaming, in the groove between the cockpit and the back deck. The blade without the paddlefloat (the "empty" blade) will extend just beyond the opposite side of the kayak. (Although it's a good idea to practice this rescue until you're fluent from either side, we'll describe it from the right.) To help remember which side of the paddle to position yourself on, use the mnemonic "back, back, back." That is, position yourself facing the *back* deck, in *back* of your cockpit, and in *back* of your paddle, with your right shoulder near the paddle shaft.

An older method that continues to work well for some kayakers, especially for shorter-legged ones, is to set up with your body in front of the paddle shaft next to the cockpit. When using this method, your upper body needs to move at an angle across the back deck and paddle shaft, with your head toward the rudder, while your left foot goes onto the extended paddle shaft and your right leg into the cockpit. The main problem with this method is the cockpit itself. People tend to get their elbows and PFDs hung up on the edges of the cockpit coaming. Those with long legs find it difficult to maneuver their feet down into the cockpit. This method of starting in front of the paddle was commonly taught in the early 1990s, but more recently the method we prefer—starting from behind the paddle—has become much more popular.

Step 4: Secure the Paddle Shaft with Hands Only Method

By firmly grasping your right hand around the paddle shaft and into the coaming behind the seat, you will be making an outrigger of your paddle. Be sure to maintain a tight grip on the paddle: The amount of stability is directly related to the immobility of the paddle shaft. If your paddle wobbles, so will your rescue platform.

For some paddlers, especially those with small hands, hanging on to the paddle can pose a challenge. If gripping the paddle is a problem for you, you might try using a sling or the Deck Rigging method of securing your paddle shaft, described later in this chapter.

Our personal preference, however, is to start by teaching the Hands Only method. We have found that it is quicker and simpler for most students under most conditions because it eliminates two steps (putting the paddle under the deck rigging and removing it afterward). We also find it more versatile because it works with any boat or paddle and does not require any extra gear, such as appropriate deck rigging, to be successful. Even in rough-water practice sessions, few of our students seem to notice any lack of stability from not having the paddle secured under the bungees. But the more options you have at your disposal, the better off you'll be, so we suggest you try both methods and see which one works best for you.

Step 5: Swim onto the Back Deck

Reach across the deck with your left hand, float your feet up to the surface or kick them out behind you, and with a final strong kick pull the kayak under your stomach as you kick forward and out of the water. Kick and pull until your belly button is centered over the boat, keeping your head slightly higher than your derriere by arching your back. Be sure to maintain some weight on the paddlefloat. If you put too much weight on the opposite side, you will tip back into the water headfirst. Some people have better luck if they first put their right ankle onto the paddle shaft (not the knee, just the *ankle*) to push off of the paddlefloat as they pull themselves across the boat. Be sure to hold on to the

Step 4: Secure the Paddle Shaft with Hands Only Method—
Hold the paddle shaft against the coaming by gripping it strongly and securely with your thumb.

Step 5: Swim onto the Back Deck—
Kick your feet out behind you and pull the kayak underneath you.

paddle shaft tightly if you try this method.

If you are having trouble getting onto the back deck, you may need to use a sling, as described in Chapter 8.

Step 6: Sea Star, One Limb at a Time

Once you're balanced on the back deck, you'll need to rotate slowly—one limb at a time—feet-first, into the cockpit. *Be sure to keep a limb and some weight on the paddlefloat throughout this entire rescue.* Have you ever seen a sea star rotate on its hub by gradually and slowly moving its limbs one at a time? Imagine your belly button sticking to the center of the back deck like a suction cup as you move first your right foot, then your left foot, across the paddle.

Step 7: Switch Legs

As your left foot controls the paddle and keeps it perpendicular to the kayak, your right foot will move into the cockpit; you will need to move your pelvic bones up and over the seat back. Your belly button needs to let up on the suction, but not much; don't use your knees for kneeling. This is not a "prayer" position so much as a "groveling on your belly" position.

Step 6: Sea Star, One Limb at a Time—
Use your feet to keep the paddlefloat perpendicular to the kayak and get your bellybutton centered on the back deck.

Step 7: Switch Legs—
Keep your paddle shaft perpendicular to your kayak, and keep weight on the paddlefloat with your left leg as you spin your right leg into the cockpit.

Step 8: Left Hand Replaces Left Foot—
Before removing your left foot from the paddle, it's important to first grab the paddle shaft with your left hand.

Step 8: Left Hand Replaces Left Foot

Before you release the paddle shaft from your left foot, you must replace it with your left hand. This is a crux move for this rescue. Because it is a long reach to grab the paddle shaft with your left hand, first move your head across the deck until it is out over the edge of the kayak on the same side as the paddlefloat. This will shorten the distance required to grab the paddle. Be sure to keep your belly button centered on the midline of the kayak. If you don't, you may find yourself slipping off the back deck to one side or the other. Also, you'll be much more stable if you make sure to grab the paddle toward the middle of the shaft, several inches or more away from the side of the kayak instead of right next to it.

Once you have a good hold on the paddle shaft and have balanced some weight onto your left hand, remove your left foot and start working it into the cockpit.

Step 9: "Corkscrew" into the Seat

Stay on your stomach as you slide both legs into the cockpit, making sure your hipbones clear the seat back without collapsing it under your hips. Start turning toward the paddlefloat,

Step 9: "Corkscrew" into the Seat—
Continue leaning on the paddlefloat as you work your other leg into the cockpit, and then twist your lower body into a seated position.

and "corkscrew" your butt down into the seat. During this entire corkscrew move, be sure to maintain your weight on your left hand on the paddle shaft and your head out over that side of the kayak. It is not uncommon for students to spin into their seats leaning away from the paddlefloat and promptly recapsize.

Step 10: Switch Hands

Keep leaning out over the paddlefloat side of the kayak as you switch your right hand for your left on the paddle shaft. Note that your head remains out to the side of the kayak. The center of the platform is the paddle shaft, not the kayak.

Step 11: Move the Paddle to the Front and Pump Out the Boat

With your right hand still out on the paddle shaft and your weight slightly off center toward that side, reach under the paddle shaft with your right hand and quickly lift the paddle up and over your head in front of you. When you do this, don't lift the paddlefloat: Leave it on the water so it continues to provide stability.

When the shaft is in front of you, your elbows and rib cage can manage to keep it in place so you can continue to lean on it for support

Step 10: Switch Hands—
Slide your right hand out onto the paddle shaft before removing your left hand.

Step 11: Move Paddle to Front and Pump Out—
Keep leaning on the paddlefloat for balance as you quickly bring the paddle up over your head and across your lap. You can continue to lean on it with your elbows as you pump out your cockpit.

while you pump the water out of the kayak. (This assumes you're using a common, handheld bilge pump; fancy foot and electric pumps are described in Chapter 2.) Don't worry about getting the kayak completely dry. When the pump starts sucking air, you are getting down to the last inch. At that point you can stop pumping because the small amount of water sloshing around in your cockpit is not enough to make your kayak unstable. If water splashes into your kayak while you pump in rough seas, you can secure the sprayskirt and then move one side of the skirt over to slide the pump down into the cockpit to reach the water you want to drain.

After you stow the pump, take the paddlefloat off your paddle and quickly deflate it, fully or partially, close the valve, tuck it under the bungees (or behind the seat) and clip it in.

In rough seas you can try paddling with your inflated paddlefloat still on your blade. This is a bit awkward, but it can provide extra stability.

The Deck Rigging Method of Paddlefloat Self-Rescue

The idea behind securing the paddle under the deck rigging is that it offers more stability, provided the deck rigging is snug enough to hold the paddle tightly in place. Those who prefer this method like the advantage of having their hands free while they are pumping out their cockpits and replacing their skirts. We have found that this method tends to work better with kayaks whose owners have spent some time customizing the rigging to accept a particular paddle width.

Standard off-the-rack bungees often provide a poor fit. If they're too loose, they won't hold the paddle in place securely. If they're too tight, then the difficulty is both securing the paddle into position to start the rescue and then removing it afterward. It can be quite awkward to pull your paddle out from behind you when you are back in your seat, facing forward in rough seas. Some kayak manufacturers are addressing these problems with additional quick-release rescue straps, and some paddlers retrofit their own kayaks to suit their

The Deck Rigging Method of securing the paddlefloat frees your hands for pumping but requires customized rigging and a constant paddle width.

needs. This method can be extremely effective as long as you are paddling your own kayak. A potential problem, however, is that your self-rescue might not work if you paddle a kayak without adequate rigging, or even if you use a paddle with a different-width blade. For these reasons, we recommend developing the Hands Only technique and your grip, or carrying a sling, so you'll have a rescue that will work with a variety of kayaks.

Fancy Flips: Waterless Righting Techniques

To minimize the amount of water that enters the cockpit while re-righting the boat during the Paddlefloat Self-Rescue (as well as for the Scramble Rescue described in Chapter 6), some paddlers are able to right their kayaks in ways that scoop so little water that there is virtually no need to pump their boats dry after reentry. These techniques probably won't work for kayaks that don't have bulkheads fore and aft.

Bow Lift Fancy Flip:
Lifting the bow from the water is an ultra-quick, albeit challenging, method for draining the water out of the cockpit before solo reentry.

The Bow Lift Fancy Flip

Roger's favorite way to get the water out of his kayak during self-rescue is the Bow Lift method. To do this, he swims to the bow after securing and inflating his paddlefloat. He grabs the bow with both hands, resting his paddle over his left shoulder to keep hold of it, and twists the boat sideways just enough to break the seal of water on the cockpit. Next he lifts the bow out of the water using an "egg-beater kick" with his feet ("like a water polo goalie," he says) and using his left hand to scull water for extra lift. The trick is to spin the boat back upright while it's still in the air, so it doesn't scoop water as it turns. This is not an easy move for many people; it helps to have Roger's long arms and upper-body strength. Also, it's much easier to do with some boats than others.

Even if you do scoop some water using the Bow Lift, you'll likely have less to pump out than if you didn't use this method, so it's worth practicing it to see if you can make it work for you and your boat. The Bow Lift is actually easier in choppy water or swell, if you can time your movements with the wave action to help you lift the bow.

Some kayakers use their paddlefloats in a variety of ways for extra flotation for lifting the bow. One instructor friend of ours, Mary, likes to straddle hers "like a witch on a broom," as she describes it. Other people grab their paddle by the throat, right next to the paddlefloat, and push off it with one hand while lifting the bow with the other. You can also lie on your back with the paddlefloat in an armpit and a leg hooked around the paddle shaft for support while you lift.

The Stern Push Fancy Flip

Another way to raise the bow so the water drains from the cockpit is to push down on the stern. This technique is also easier with some

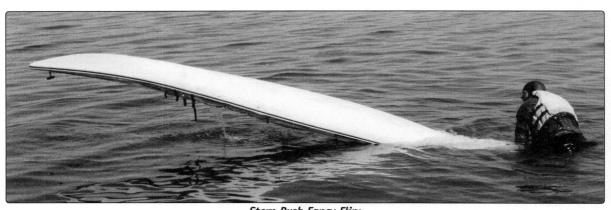

Stern Push Fancy Flip:
Pushing down on the stern might raise the cockpit out of the water far enough to drain the kayak, depending on your mass and the volume of the stern.

REAL LIFE RESCUES

Happily Ever After

"It was a calm and sunny day . . . " Our friend Robert's story began like so many of the accident reports we had read about over the years in *Sea Kayaker* magazine. He had taken many classes and trips with us before moving recently to Kailua Beach, Hawaii. "I was new to the islands and had no one to paddle with, so I decided to go out by myself to the Mokulua Islands. They're barely a mile offshore."

He was paddling his closed-deck sea kayak. Since it was relatively calm with only small waves breaking on the outer reefs, he decided to paddle through a channel to have a look beyond the islands. The swell was very friendly, and he was enjoying being out on the open ocean with sea turtles popping up around him. When returning through the channel, however, he was surprised by a large wave.

"It dumped me quickly. I missed my roll a couple of times and bailed out." After wet exiting, he took a quick look around and saw that although he was being pushed by wind and current toward calmer waters, he was still well offshore. At first he wasn't sure what to do next. In many years of paddling, he'd never actually had to rescue himself in a real-life situation.

But since he had practiced rescues countless times in our classes, his body seemed to know what to do. "I just pulled out my paddlefloat and started the self-rescue like we had always practiced. Everything went smoothly. I climbed back in my boat and finished the paddle back to my house without a problem." End of story.

Although his story began like a typical accident report, it had a happy ending. But not because Robert got lucky. He made his own luck. No one read about Robert's misadventure in the pages of *Sea Kayaker,* because he had taken the time to learn and practice basic rescues. He continues to paddle happily ever after in Hawaii.

Roger + Jan

boats than others, and paddlers who have more mass will find it easier to sink the stern. When doing this flip, be careful to hang on to your kayak, as it tends to squirt away from you. And if you have a rudder, be careful that it doesn't hit you in the face.

Paddlefloat Self-Rescue Practice Tips

There is no substitute for deep-water rescue practice. In our classes, however, we introduce the Paddlefloat Rescue on shore and in the shallows first. This way, students have the opportunity to work out the awkward body mechanics while warm and dry on the beach. The "sea star" can be set up and worked through on the sand, and then again in shallow water until you get your belly-button suction down and start to feel out the balance points. As important as it is to keep one limb out on the paddle shaft at all times, the transitions from leg to hand and then from one hand to the other are especially challenging, and your head position during those transitions will be critical. We've found that when we have students work out these details on shore and in the shallows first, their open-water rescues are much more efficient.

When you do move to deep water, make sure you're in a protected area near shore at first without any offshore wind or currents, so you can swim yourself to shore or have a partner rescue you if your reentry doesn't work. There are further rough-water practice tips in Chapter 4.

The Paddlefloat Self-Rescue is a great first rescue for someone getting started. It requires some extra gear and lots of practice to stay sharp, but no matter how good your other rescues get, it can always be used as a backup tool during your sea kayaking adventures.

The paddlefloat device itself can also come in handy in situations besides a reentry. We've used it as a stabilizing outrigger while towing paddlers who needed help staying upright in cases of seasickness or other disabling maladies. We realize that there are still a few paddlers who have yet to recognize it as a viable rough-water device, but we're convinced that it's an essential safety tool.

▪ The T Rescue

Whether in practice or real life, whenever someone capsizes and ends up in the water around us, the rescue we find ourselves performing most often *by far* is the T Rescue. From a novice tipping over while practicing braces in flat water to an advanced student on the open coast or a paddling buddy who misses a roll in a churning sea cave—all of them receive T Rescues as a matter of course. It's the quickest, easiest, and most versatile way we've found to get a swimmer back in a kayak *and ready to paddle*. (This assumes, of course, that the kayak has a rear bulkhead; otherwise a TX Rescue, described later in this chapter, will be necessary.)

The T Rescue is a two-person, two-part reentry. While in the T-position, the rescuer first lifts the bow of the capsized kayak, quickly dumping the water out of the cockpit. Next the rescuer stabilizes the kayak while the swimmer climbs back aboard. Once back in the kayak, the (ex) swimmer is ready to paddle with no need for additional pumping, since the water was emptied prior to reentering.

Step by Step

T Rescue

Step 1: Form the T

Remember: Before initiating any rescue, take a moment to check the swimmer's state of mind. A panicky swimmer could capsize you, so don't get too close until you've calmed him down. Also, remind the swimmer (frequently during the rescue) to be sure to hang on to his kayak and paddle. A good sign that a swimmer has his wits about him, in fact, is if he is still hanging on to his gear as you approach. A hysterical swimmer will likely be splashing about wildly or trying to scramble onto his kayak while his paddle floats away.

To get yourself into the T-position quickly and efficiently, your approach will be important. You want to pick a route that leads you quickly and directly to the swimmer's bow (the front of the kayak), without a lot of extra maneuvering. In our classes we sometimes see beginners paddling around in wild circles trying to get to the bow; or they may get mixed up and grab the stern. This can be rather amusing to watch—for everyone except the swimmer. You can be quite certain that your swimmer will *not* be amused with your lack of boat control as he bobs about like an ice cube in the cold water. Practice the Capture the Bow technique described below until you can get to the bow consistently on your first pass.

Go quickly, but don't worry too much about getting to the bow at a perfectly perpendicular angle. When you can reach the bow, pull it toward you and lean onto it with both hands; then use it as a pivot point to lever your kayak around into the T-position. It can be difficult to tell bow from stern on some kayaks, especially when they are upside down, so look for the foot-brace screws along the side of the kayak toward the bow end.

It can be a challenge to keep track of your paddle, not to mention the swimmer's paddle, during this or any other assisted rescue. We find it works best to have the swimmer keep hold of his own paddle until the point at which you are ready

T Rescue: Step 1: Form the T—
Firmly grasping the overturned bow with two hands, leverage your kayak into a right angle with the other kayak.

Step 2: Lift the Bow—
Lean on the bow of the overturned kayak with your right hand, then lean back, pulling the bow up onto your lap with your left hand as the swimmer pushes down on the stern.

to stabilize his boat for reentry. As a rescuer, you'll have enough on your hands with the two kayaks and your own paddle. Also, if you capsize during the rescue while holding the swimmer's paddle, then he may not have access to it if he needs to perform a solo reentry.

When performing a T Rescue, we think it's best to keep your paddle across your lap, just below the bottom of your PFD and against your stomach. Keeping the paddle in your lap is the best method we've found for keeping track of it in rough water, except for leashing it. The potential downside with a leash, however, is that it can cause problems during rescues if you or the swimmer gets tangled in it, or if it gets in the way of maneuvering the kayaks.

Another method is stashing the paddle under your bungees. This may work in calm water, but in rougher conditions the paddle sometimes ends up either getting in the way or else washing away from under the bungees while you are focused on the rescue. We've also found that if you capsize while giving a T Rescue, having your paddle in your lap allows you to grab it for an Eskimo Roll or other rescue instead of getting it tangled up in your bungees or a leash.

Step 2: Lift the Bow

Once you're in the T-position, you'll need to lift the swimmer's bow from the water and place it across your lap. We've found that this is much easier if you can get the swimmer to help by pushing down on the stern of the overturned boat while you lift. So if he hasn't already, ask the swimmer to move to his stern, and remind him again to keep hold of his boat. If the overturned boat has a rudder, the swimmer should also be careful not to cut his hands on any sharp edges.

Lifting the kayak can be unstable, particularly if you try to lift it with only one hand. Instead, reach over your paddle and put whichever hand is nearest to the capsized kayak about a foot or two up along its keel line (if the kayak is on your right side, it will be your right hand). Lean on the capsized kayak for support, and use your other hand (the left) to reach *across* your body and under the capsized kayak to find the tip of the bow. *The trick is that you'll be using your left hand to do the lifting while leaning on the overturned kayak with your right hand for support.* When you are ready to lift, have the swimmer shove his weight down on the stern while you pull up on the bow and drag it across your lap, using the leverage of your body rocking back upright to lift the bow.

If you are having trouble lifting the bow, try turning the capsized kayak back upright first. The bow will then be easier to grab, but the boat will be full of water and heavy, so you'll want to flip it back over to drain the water as soon as possible.

This extra step of turning the kayak upright and then back over takes more time, but it's a good option to have up your sleeve.

A more advanced technique for lifting an overturned kayak requires confidence in your own stability. Leaning on the hull of the swimmer's kayak, tilt your own kayak far enough over to scoop the upside-down bow into the edge of your cockpit coaming. Then by rocking your kayak back upright and raising that edge of your coaming, you can pry up the other bow with leverage much like that applied by a bottle opener popping a cold one. This method can work well, but it requires good balance and practice to do it without tipping yourself over in the process.

Instead of having the swimmer help with the reentry, some paddlers advocate having him move to the rescuer's bow and hang there, supposedly to keep him out of the way yet under surveillance. In our experience, however, most swimmers are eager to help with their own rescues and prefer to maintain contact with their own kayaks and paddles. Besides, the reentry is faster when two people are working at it. If a swimmer doesn't seem capable of helping, it might be better to get him directly back into his kayak before it's drained, because he may not be comfortable or even safe in the water.

Step 3: Drain the Cockpit

When the kayak is across your lap, most of the water will have drained out. You could turn it back over now, but you'll just scoop water back into the cockpit. To avoid this, you'll need to lift the cockpit higher out of the water before you flip it. There are two main ways to do this, the Drag method and the King Kong, or Weightlifter, method.

With the Drag, you lift and drag the kayak across your lap using both hands and forearms until you can reach the empty cockpit's coaming. Getting the upturned boat this high on your own kayak keeps the overturned one from scooping water back into its cockpit when you rotate it right-side up.

Jan prefers the Drag, but Roger likes the King Kong method because it is quicker, although

Step 3: Drain the Cockpit Using the Drag Method—
Slide the kayak across your lap until you can reach the cockpit.

Optional Step 3:
Drain the Cockpit Using the King Kong Method—
Lift the bow up onto your shoulder before you right it so that it's high enough to avoid scooping water into the cockpit.

it requires more brawn. He lifts the bow of the kayak overhead like a weightlifter to drain it. If you turn and face the kayak while lifting it for a King Kong, you can rest it on your shoulder (the left one if you're lifting from the right), which is easier and more stable than lifting it overhead. *Safety note:* Be careful when trying this gorilla technique, because the force required, combined with the twisting of your torso, can be hard on your lower back.

Step 4: Right the Kayak

Let the swimmer know when you will roll his kayak and in which direction so that he can help. Or he can just let the kayak rotate in his hands and manage the rudder, if there is one.

Step 5: Get the Boats Parallel, Facing Bow to Stern

Slide the empty kayak back into the water and use the bow as a pivot point again, leaning onto it with both hands and using it to lever your kayak around parallel, facing in opposite directions, with your bow toward its stern. Then walk your hands down the empty kayak to its cockpit, where you will stabilize it in the next step.

Facing opposite directions will make it easier for both of you to perform the next couple of steps of the rescue. Lifting your paddle over the other kayak at this point and resting it on the two decks of the kayaks makes it easier to move the kayak and keep track of the paddle. As you move the kayaks to parallel, remind the swimmer again to hang on to his boat, so you don't pull it out of his hands in the process.

Step 6: Stabilize for Reentry

When the two kayaks are parallel, the swimmer should move (hand over hand, remembering to maintain contact with his kayak the entire time) to the area just behind his own cockpit on the opposite side of his kayak from you. Take the swimmer's paddle, nest the two paddles into a bridge across the front of both cockpits, and lean over the paddles. Firmly grasp the swimmer's cockpit coaming with a hand on each side, near the front, right by the thigh braces if there are any. Don't block the cockpit, but do lean all your weight onto his kayak. We like the expression *pit to pit*, referring to putting your armpit across the front of his cockpit. If the boats had ended up facing the same direction in the previous step instead of bow to stern, you'd now be in the way—hanging on to the back deck where he needs to climb up—or you'd be too far forward to get a good grip. Although it is possible to continue if the kayaks face the same direction, it is awkward.

Step 5: Get the Boats Parallel, Facing Bow to Stern— *Use both hands to leverage yourself around the empty kayak until both kayaks are parallel.*

Step 6: Stabilize for Reentry— *Lean onto the empty kayak "pit-to-pit" across the paddle bridge for secure support.*

Step 7: Swim onto the Back Deck—
The swimmer should kick his feet out behind him and pull the deck underneath his stomach.

Step 8: "Corkscrew" Reentry—
The swimmer should lean onto the rescuer's kayak and turn toward the rescuer.

Step 7: Swim onto the Back Deck

The swimmer then kicks his feet out behind himself and pulls his kayak under his stomach, pushing the kayak down with his elbows while lunging onto the back deck. He should reach across to grab your kayak as soon as possible to help stabilize the raft.

If the swimmer has trouble getting onto the back deck, you can try reaching over and grabbing the shoulder of his PFD to help boost him up. If that doesn't work, pull out your sling, as described in Chapter 7.

Step 8: "Corkscrew" Reentry

Remind the now ex-swimmer to stay on his stomach to keep his center of gravity low, as he rotates his head toward the stern of his kayak and begins working his legs and hips into his cockpit. Once his hips are past the seat back, he can corkscrew his body around to sit his butt back into his seat. During the reentry procedure, the swimmer must be careful not to collapse the seat back or he'll end up sitting on it. He should also continue to brace a hand on the rescue kayak for support, and be sure to corkscrew facing *toward* the rescuer.

As the rescuer, you should continue stabilizing his kayak until he has secured his sprayskirt and recovered his wits. If you let go before he is ready, he may capsize again. Separate smoothly and avoid giving each other a big push sideways. When the rescue is finished, keep the kayaks parallel and hand-walk backward down each other's bows, watching for loose or dragging gear or any sign of instability of either partner.

T Rescue Practice Tips

So that our students' first practice rescues go more smoothly and efficiently, we have developed several drills for them to practice ahead of time. Occasionally we see rescuers paddling in circles trying to figure out how to get to someone else's bow for a rescue. It is better to learn to maneuver efficiently before anyone dumps into cold water. For this, we like to play a game

REAL LIFE RESCUES

Talking through the T

"Hang on to your boat," I call out instinctively as I near Paul's overturned kayak. These are generally the first words out of my mouth when approaching any capsize, followed quickly, if necessary, with "and grab your paddle." Jan and I both say this even before asking, "Are you okay?" because in our book, a swimmer who has let go of his gear is *not* okay, so the question is moot until he has secured his boat and paddle.

With Paul, my reminders about gear and questions about his well–being are mere formalities. He has wet exited under perfect control without ever letting go of paddle or boat, and his familiar sheepish grin coupled with a jolly "Roger that, Roger" tell me that although dripping wet, both he and his dry wit are intact.

Whether or not your swimmer is as well practiced as Paul, if the T Rescue is to work smoothly, it helps to have good communication between the two rescuers: the one in the boat and the swimmer in the water who's helping rescue himself. We've found that a few well-timed comments helps keep the rescuers in sync, acting as the grease that allows the reentry to glide smoothly and efficiently from start to finish. Most of this talking is done by the paddler in the kayak, who's usually in a better position to take charge of or orchestrate the reentry. The basic idea is for the person in the boat to anticipate each next step and talk the swimmer through it. Over the years, we've talked so many students through so many T Rescues in so many conditions that we seem to shift into automatic, like pushing the PLAY button on our prerecorded rescue message. Perhaps a good way to give a sense of the phrases we favor is to continue with the rest of this example, focusing on the things we routinely say when doing a rescue.

Like most experienced kayakers, Paul already has a hold of his boat and paddle, and he's moving toward his stern, hand over hand to maintain contact with his kayak. As I grab his bow and maneuver my kayak into the T-position, I fast-forward past the reminders we often give less practiced paddlers: "Go to the back of your boat," and, "Keep hanging on."

"Get ready to push down on your stern when I'm ready to lift it," I do tell him next. I want to get our timing together, so he doesn't start pushing on his boat until I'm in position. When I've got a good hold on the bow, I say, "Okay, push down now." Some people like to count to three to better time the swimmer's push with their own bow lift. If the swimmer is moving slowly and isn't ready to help, I sometimes just ask him to hold on to his kayak and I lift it by myself rather than wait. This assumes that the boats are lightly loaded for a day trip and that I'm feeling strong enough to lift the bow without help. With an expedition-loaded kayak or if I'm feeling tired, I'll wait for help.

With Paul giving his stern a good shove, I'm able to lift his bow quickly to my shoulder, drain the cockpit, and slide his boat back into the water. Out of habit, I glance out to sea to make sure no waves are coming, but we are just outside the mouth of a large, protected sea cave on the north side of Mendocino Bay and the ocean has been uncharacteristically calm all day long. It wasn't a wave or rough seas that capsized Paul on this occasion. He was experimenting with a fancy turning stroke we'd just shown him, a Cross-Bow Draw, when his paddle got tangled in kelp and tripped him up. So this reentry is a routine mirror image of the many, many T Rescues we've both practiced, and we're both on autopilot.

I pivot my kayak parallel and start moving hand over hand toward his cockpit. Here again, being an experienced paddler, Paul is already moving hand over hand back toward his cockpit. But sometimes we need to remind a swimmer, "Come on up to your cockpit now, and keep hanging on to your boat."

When Paul reaches his cockpit, I say, "Give me your paddle now." If the swimmer is stressed and starts trying to climb onto his kayak before I've had a chance to lean across the paddles and stabilize it, I'll say, "Wait a sec. Don't climb up until I've got a hold of your boat." Then: "Okay, I'm ready. Kick your feet out behind you and swim up onto your back deck."

But Paul needs no direction, and we revert to shorthand. He watches me and waits until I have his paddle stowed and I'm steadying his boat. "Ready?" he asks.

I nod. "Gotcha." And he swims up onto his back deck.

Once a swimmer is on his deck, the next several reminders make the reentry easier for both of us by nipping common problems in the bud. "Reach over and put an arm on my boat," I'll ask him, "to help me stabilize the boats." But Paul is already leaning on my deck, making my job of stabilization twice as easy, so I remain mute. I see that he is also being careful to lift his hips before sliding into his cockpit, avoiding the common problem of collapsing his seat back and sitting on it, which raises the swimmer's center of gravity and often leads to recapsize. But Paul saves me the trouble of having to say, "Careful. Watch out for your seat." With less experienced paddlers, it is good to give this reminder just *before* they start sliding their legs in. And then, *before* they start to corkscrew back into the seat, I say, "Remember to turn toward me," so they'll keep leaning on my kayak to help stabilize the raft.

Instead of giving Paul these unnecessary reminders, I listen to him apologize as he corkscrews smoothly into his seat, embarrassed for having capsized in calm water and making me have to do a rescue. Far from being perturbed, I'm happy to see him experimenting with new strokes, even if they lead to a capsize. And I'm thankful for all the rescue practice he's done, practically rescuing himself and making my job as the rescuer so much easier.

Roger

called Capture the Bow. Have your partner paddle several boat lengths away from you and then stop as if she has capsized. See how quickly you can get to her bow. The object is to paddle directly to her bow and grab it *on the first pass* without any extra maneuvering, backing up, or circling. Take turns paddling away from each other at different distances and in different directions, until you are consistently able to make clean grabs.

Once you have grabbed your partner's bow, maneuvering the two kayaks around each other is one of the more challenging aspects of this rescue. The trick is to get the idea of how to use both hands to pivot quickly around the overturned kayak; then the other steps will fall into place. To practice this while you are both still in your kayaks, take turns grabbing each other's bow and pivoting back and forth from a perpendicular T-position to parallel facing each other, using both of your hands and boat lean to move your boat quickly and efficiently.

Before moving into deep-water rescue practice, we've had great success when students start out practicing rescues in water no more than waist deep. That way the "swimmer" can stand up next to her boat (staying much warmer in cold water); if the rescue goes awry, she can just wade to shore. The person pretending to be the swimmer can also help by anchoring the kayaks so they don't drift away while you work out hand positions and lower-body leveraging. Once you get your chops down and can go through the rescue fairly smoothly, then you can move it out into deep water.

For sea kayaks with rear bulkheads, the T Rescue is a quick and effective assisted rescue that can be used in a wide range of conditions. Practice will make its execution second nature. Almost anyone can be talked through the procedure as long as they keep calm. People who panic in the water or use kayaks without bulkheads, especially loaded kayaks without bulkheads, will require different rescue techniques (see Variations on a T Theme, below).

■ Variations on a T Theme: Alternate Model Ts and Other Assisted Rescues

As much as we prefer the standard T Rescue, there are times when it just doesn't apply. Expanding your rescue repertoire will allow you to deal more effectively with a wider variety of situations. Once you are comfortable with the standard T Rescue, it will be easy to add the following variations—the TX, Rafted T, and Reenter and Pump—to your bag of tricks.

TX Rescue

As noted above, a T Rescue only works on kayaks with rear bulkheads. So what do you do if a bulkheadless buddy ends up in the drink? Time to dust off the old TX Rescue. Over the past few decades, bulkheads have become fairly standard on many sea-touring kayaks. Before then, float bags were commonly used for flotation, and the TX or Boat Over Boat Rescue was the norm. It is still a good rescue to know, because there are a fair number of sans-bulkheads kayaks on the water.

Basically the TX starts out like a T, with the rescuer lifting the bow of the capsized kayak. But with no rear bulkhead behind the seat, the stern will fill with water when the bow is lifted. To empty both ends, the rescuer must drag the kayak all the way across her lap (hopefully with some help from the swimmer) in order to raise the stern and teeter-totter the kayak back and forth across her cockpit. Then the rescuer stabilizes the drained kayak for the swimmer to reenter, as in the standard T Rescue. Note that float bags (or a sea sock) are necessary for this rescue to work, because it can be extremely difficult to rescue a swamped kayak without some form of flotation.

Step by Step

TX Rescue

Step 1: Check In and T-Position

This rescue starts and finishes exactly like the T Rescue. The only difference is the extra step of draining the stern. The rescuer goes to the bow and maneuvers into the T-position.

Step 2: Lift the Bow

As in the T, the swimmer moves to the stern of his kayak to push down on it as the assistant lifts the bow with two hands. Each person in the rescue hangs on to his or her own paddle.

Step 3: Drag the Kayak into the X-Position

This is where the TX differs from the T Rescue. The capsized kayak needs to be dragged all the way across the rescuer's kayak until the two cockpits meet and the stern can be lifted. This is the X-position, and the kayak on top needs to be rocked bow-down, bow-up—like a teeter-totter—until the water empties out of both ends.

The more help you can get from the swimmer, the easier it will be to drag the kayak all the way across your lap and lift the stern full of water. One way for him to help is to go to the opposite side of your cockpit (being careful to maintain contact with the boats) and help drag the kayak by pulling on the bow while pushing off your kayak with his feet for added leverage. Optionally, the swimmer can also stay at the stern and help lift it.

Step 4: Stabilize for Reentry

Once the kayak is drained, it is righted and dragged back into the water into the bow-to-stern position. Then it is stabilized, and the rest of the rescue goes back to the same steps as a T Rescue: The swimmer hands off his paddle, and the rescuer reaches across the paddles to stabilize the kayak while the swimmer bellies up onto his back deck and corkscrews back into his cockpit by turning toward the rescuer.

Kayaks without bulkheads are great, in our minds, for paddlers with bombproof Eskimo Rolls who don't come out of their boats. When it comes to us having to rescue someone from the water, however, bulkheads front and rear are a welcome sight. Sure, they add expense and weight, and they take away gear space or even leak, but TX Rescues are a lot of work no matter how well the float bags may fit. If the boats involved are fiberglass, the extra weight of water in the stern when you rock it across your kayak could be enough to damage the fiberglass decks. If the capsized kayak is loaded with camping gear, you can forget the TX, whereas we have been able to perform successful standard T Rescues on loaded boats with bulkheads. With loaded kayaks, you may have no option but to do the Reenter and Pump Rescue, described below. Our favorite kind of kayak for a TX Rescue is a plastic river kayak—lightweight, short, and indestructible.

TX Rescue:
The swimmer helps to drag the kayak into the X-position.

Rafted (Assisted) T Rescue

Essentially the Rafted T Rescue is a standard T Rescue that involves a second rescue boater who supports and stabilizes you while you manipulate the overturned kayak to drain the water and then allow a swimmer to climb back aboard. This is an especially good rescue to use in rough seas if you feel unstable while trying to perform a standard T Rescue (assuming, of course, that—as with all forms of T Rescue—the boat being rescued has a rear bulkhead). It involves some extra teamwork, but if both people can maneuver their kayaks and work well together, this can be a powerful rescue.

Step by Step

Rafted T Rescue

Step 1: Check In and T-Position

As with the other assisted rescues, start talking with the swimmer as you approach. Maneuver into the T-position with the swimmer's upturned kayak.

Step 2: Stabilize the First Kayak

The second rescue boater can join in to stabilize you as soon as you are in the T-position. It is most efficient if your stabilizer can come in facing the same direction as you and firmly grasp your cockpit coaming from *behind* your seat. His paddle will be behind you and in front of him, and it's helpful if he can quickly nest your paddle with his to leave your hands free to do the rescue.

Step 3: Lift the Bow

You can now proceed as with a standard T Rescue, lifting the bow onto your lap. Optionally, if you are having trouble lifting the bow, the second rescuer can stabilize you while you tilt your kayak far enough to get the rim of your cockpit coaming under the bow of the overturned kayak and pry it up by rocking your kayak back upright.

Step 4: Drain the Kayak

If you are having trouble lifting the bow of the kayak high enough to drain the water from the cockpit and spinning it without scooping more

Rafted (Assisted) T Rescue:
A second rescuer helps to stabilize the first kayaker and assists in lifting the bow of the overturned kayak.

water, your stabilizer may be able to move forward to help raise or drag the bow across. If he moves forward, he'll need to bring the paddles forward in front of both of your laps. This extra help can take a little more communication, but it can be highly effective, especially if you're trying to drain a two-person kayak.

Step 5: Stabilize for Reentry

You will want to take the swimmer's paddle and prepare to stabilize her kayak by grasping the swimmer's cockpit at both sides of the front of the coaming. Pass her paddle to your stabilizer; he can nest it with the other two. The swimmer will reenter in the same way as with the T Rescue: by kicking to propel her upper body onto her kayak and then corkscrewing her legs back into her seat while you continue to stabilize.

Working out the support method that will work best for your paddling cohorts will require good communication skills and practice. Try this with different companions playing out the different roles. We have found the Rafted T can also be very useful while practicing or demonstrating a rescue with our students. The raft may contain an instructor coaching a student through the rescue, or it could be made up of a student observing the instructor.

We recommend this rescue for choppy seas when there are multiple skilled boaters around. It can also be used as an effective teaching tool.

Reenter and Pump

Also called the Side by Side Rescue, the Reenter and Pump is basically the second half of the T Rescue; you don't take the time to first lift the bow and drain the cockpit. The overturned kayak is righted, full of water, and stabilized to allow the swimmer to get back into the cockpit. Then the water is pumped out. This can be useful in situations where you might have trouble lifting the bow, perhaps with bulkheadless boats, in rough seas, or with heavily laden expedition kayaks. You might also use it if you need to get a cold or injured swimmer back into her boat *pronto*, without even taking the few extra seconds necessary to first lift the bow using a T Rescue.

Step by Step

Reenter and Pump

Step 1: Check In

As with all rescues, approach the swimmer with caution until her panic level can be assessed.

Step 2: Right the Overturned Kayak

Get side by side, parallel to the capsized kayak. The reentry phase will be easier to perform if you are in the bow-to-stern position, as with the T Rescue. To right the boat, reach over the hull to grasp it by the cockpit coaming (or the farthest you can reach across it), then push down on the near side as you pull up on the far side. Your paddle should be across your lap. If she is capable, get the swimmer to help you right her boat, and remind her to hang on to her kayak.

Reenter and Pump: Step 2:
***Right the Overturned Kayak**—Grasp the kayak by the cockpit coaming and push down on the near side while pulling up on the far side.*

Step 4: Pump Out the Kayak—
Pumping out the kayak is twice as fast using both pumps.

Step 3: Stabilize for Reentry

With the kayak righted, parallel to yours, follow the same steps as for a T Rescue. The swimmer hands off her paddle; you reach across the paddles to stabilize; and the swimmer bellies up onto her back deck, grabs both kayaks, swings her legs into her cockpit, and corkscrews toward you into her seat.

Step 4: Pump Out the Kayak

The swimmer is now back in a boat full of water. Both of you need to start pumping. If the ex-swimmer is taking on water from spray or chop, get her sprayskirt mostly onto the coaming and then put the pumps down the sides of the cockpit, between the skirt and the coaming. If there is another paddler in your group, encourage her to come alongside and use her pump as well.

The more pumps you can use, the sooner you can get the boat pumped out, and the sooner you can start paddling again.

Although we prefer using T Rescues so the swimmer can reenter a dry boat that is ready to paddle, the Reenter and Pump is a good alternative if you are unable to lift the bow or if you need to get someone out of the water in a hurry. Of course, that person will still be sitting in a cockpit full of water, but at least her upper body won't be immersed. Getting back in the cockpit quickly can be a great relief to a swimmer who is hypothermic, scared, or injured. Overall, however, this rescue takes longer than a T Rescue, because pumping the water out of a kayak is generally much slower than dumping it out.

REAL LIFE RESCUES

Southerly Blow at Point Lobos

Picture a magnificent granite headland reaching deep into the Pacific's prevailing northwest swell. Windswept cypress trees accentuate the high weathered rocks, while the clearest cold blue waves sweep through a skirt of kelp beds, spraying deep into craggy coves. Point Lobos is the epitome of raw, powerful beauty. We have run many an epic trip here, where getting humbled by the sea is just part of the overall experience.

This time we arrive knowing that the forecast calls for southerly winds, an incoming system. The swell is the usual 4 to 6 feet out of the northwest. It's early summer, so the kelp has recovered from the winter storms and helps buffer the swell in some places. On this particular trip we are seven strong paddlers with varying degrees of rough water training. Mitch and Carl are in new kayaks on their first open coast paddle. Shabbir, Buck, and Ted are veterans of the open coast with gear they know and trust. Roger and myself are to be the leaders of the day. Generally Roger leads and I bring up the rear, checking up on people and encouraging them through the rough spots. We launch from the north side of the point, expecting to reassess our plans at the point and decide whether to beat into it or head back in the lee of the point. It's still well before lunch when we arrive at the tip. Conditions seem favorable to continue; the wind "will just blow us back to this point," we kid ourselves as we discuss the southerly–wind forecast.

Lunch is just outside the marine reserve on its extreme south end, in the lee of yet another craggy cliff of Carmel. We launch after our meal, choosing a wide path away from the point, because by now we do see whitecaps blowing across the water from the south.

Carl has trouble with his boat tracking in the stiff wind, while Mitch finds that the spearing of his bow through the waves makes him feel as if he's paddling deep into a dish of spaghetti, long strands of kelp dragging over his front deck. Unfamiliar with their new boats in rough seas, they suddenly both capsize. Roger heads for one, I toward the other. Roger beats everyone to Carl and starts a T Rescue, calling for Buck and Shabbir to help tow his rescue raft away from the rocks. I get to Mitch right behind Ted, who is just pulling into the T-position and calling out that he feels very unstable in the chop. I position next to Ted for the Assisted T. Everyone works very quickly. Ted and Mitch finish up and I consider asking Ted to continue to stabilize while I tow, but the other group is heading back toward shore. I hope that going with the direction of the swell will keep Mitch's spearing bow from digging in. Luckily, this is what happens, and Mitch paddles quite adeptly away from the point. Once again a safe distance from the rocks, the two groups pull together and decide on an alternative plan.

Once on shore we find out that the two groups had used different strategies to deal with the reentries. Roger, quite stable in the wind chop, asked for towing assistance to keep from blowing into the rocks. Shabbir and Buck had towed the reentry in progress by attaching to Roger's bow toggle. In contrast, I had responded to Ted's request for stabilizing with the Assisted T, comparing the progress of his well-practiced technique to the speed of drift toward the rocks. It is a judgment call on how best to use the skilled paddlers in a group to accomplish a successful reentry; someone has to make the call and direct the process quickly.

"It will just blow us back to this point" had turned into "it just about blew us back *into this point*." If we hadn't been able to perform quick, efficient rescues (and gotten lucky), those cold blue waves would have stuffed our soft little bodies right into the magnificent granite crevices. Previous practice, teamwork, and careful boat handling by strong paddlers averted our being eaten alive by Point Lobos and the power of the Pacific.

British Style (Between Boat) Reentry

Rather than an entire rescue, this style of reentry refers *only* to the part where the swimmer climbs back into his cockpit. Therefore it can be used as an alternate way to get back into a boat after using any form of T Rescue described previously (standard T Rescue, TX, or Rafted T), or it can be a slight variation on the Reenter and Pump. We don't see this form of reentry used often on our stretch of the West Coast, but it has apparently been a long-standing staple for British paddlers. Although it is an option that can work for any kayak, it seems particularly well suited for reentering the smaller cockpit openings common on many British boats. It might also be a good rescue to try if you're wearing big rubber boots (more on this later).

Basically, after draining the kayak (or not), the rescuer stabilizes the swimmer's kayak as in a T Rescue. Instead of climbing onto the back deck on your belly from *beside* the boats and then corkscrewing into the cockpit, however, you climb onto your back deck from *between* the kayaks and stay on your backside, *facing upward*, the entire time. Since there is less room to spin your body around in a small cockpit, one advantage to this reentry is that it skips the corkscrew maneuver.

Step by Step
Between Boat Reentry

Step 1: Orient the Swimmer between the Boats

After the rescuer dumps the water out of the cockpit using some form of T Rescue (or leaving the water in if you are doing a Reenter and Pump) and stabilizes your kayak with the boats facing bow to stern, give him your paddle and move between the kayaks, putting one arm over the top of each deck. In steep chop the use of this reentry may be limited, because of the potential for harm with a swimmer between the kayaks. Adding a drogue or sea anchor may allow the kayaks to swing into the direction of the wind waves and reduce the degree of side-to-side smashing.

Step 2: Get onto the Back Deck

Before you start to get in, have the rescuer stabilize your boat, holding firmly to both sides of your cockpit coaming, as with any variation of the T Rescue, with his arms over the tops of the paddle shafts and the kayaks facing bow to stern.

With an arm over each of the kayaks, pull the two boats together as you raise your feet into your cockpit. (Raising the feet in this manner is what makes this rescue helpful for swimmers who need to drain their rubber boots.) Here's a tip: Lay your head and shoulders back as you squeeze the two kayaks together and wriggle your bum up onto your back deck. Some people find this maneuver quite awkward, a little like pushing rope.

Step 3: Slide into the Cockpit

Once your lower body is on your kayak, slide satisfyingly into your cockpit.

This between-boats-backside style of reentry might be a good option for kayakers with small cockpits (and big boots). Some paddlers swear by it, especially agile ones, and find it easier to perform than the typical New World "belly-crawl-and-corkscrew" maneuver. Many others, however, find it extremely awkward. The only way to discover if it works well for you is to practice. As a rescuer it might also be a good idea to familiarize yourself with it, so you'll know what to expect if you ever need to rescue a bailed-out Brit who begins scrambling up "backward" from between the boats.

Jan demonstrates this rescue with rubber boots as a "proof of concept". However, she never actually wears rain boots when paddling.

British Style (Between Boat) Reentry:
The swimmer slides in between the two boats, leans back while squeezing the boats together for support, then wriggles onto the back deck and into her kayak.

■ Chapter 6
Expanding Your Repertoire

- ■ Scramble
- ■ Reenter and Roll
- ■ Eskimo Bow Rescues
- ■ Eskimo Rolls

Expanding your repertoire of rescue skills takes time both on and *in* the water. Experienced paddlers sometimes refer to their "bag of tricks" when describing their collection of rescue skills. The more tricks in your bag, the more options you have, and the more quickly and efficiently you can deal with a variety of capsize scenarios. If you have been out practicing your Paddlefloat and T Rescues enough that these basic reentries are going quickly and smoothly, you might be ready for the next step. The techniques in this chapter are some of the quicker ways to recover from a capsize, and they are also some of the more challenging ones. Whether you are able to master them all or not, experimenting with them can help make you more comfortable in or out of your boat and give you a better understanding of your limits.

■ Scramble (Cowboy) Reentry

One of our personal favorites, the Scramble is among the fastest solo reentries in the book. It can be an excellent self-rescue in places like surf zones or rock gardens, where it may be difficult for a partner to come help you, or where you may not have time to rig a paddlefloat between waves. Basically, you climb onto your back deck, straddle your kayak as if sitting on a horse, shinny up to your cockpit, and sit down—using no gear except the paddle in your hand. It is not an easy rescue for beginners to master, but for intermediate and advanced paddlers it can be an especially quick alternative to a Paddlefloat Self-Rescue (though it's generally more difficult for long-legged people with smaller cockpits). Our recommendation, however, would still be to carry a paddlefloat as a backup, regardless of how bomber your Scramble or Eskimo Roll may be.

Step by Step

Scramble

Step 1: Climb onto the Back Deck

As always, hang on to your boat. If you're in the surf or near rocks, position yourself on the upwave side, or point the bow into the waves so the waves don't knock your boat into you or smash you against a rock. Flip the boat over quickly, as described for the Paddlefloat Self-Rescue, to minimize the amount of water you take on. Next you need to get up onto your back deck. This is the first of three challenging crux moves. The difficulty is getting up onto the back deck without logrolling the kayak. The easiest way to do this is to start somewhere just behind the hatch, depending on your boat. (Note that the farther back you go, the easier it will be to climb onto your boat—until you run into the rudder, if you have one—but the farther you will have to crawl to reach your cockpit and complete the rescue.) Face your boat, kick your legs out behind you on the surface as in other rescues, and launch your torso across the deck while you pull the kayak underneath you. The trick is to get enough of your body across the deck to reach a point where you are balanced on your belly and not rolling the boat back on top of you.

With a good sense of balance and a lot of practice, some people are able to climb onto the back deck right behind the cockpit or even right over it, minimizing the "scramble" part of scootching along the kayak.

Step 2: Straddle the Kayak

The second crux move is maintaining your balance over the centerline while you rotate your body to throw your leg over the kayak as if mounting a horse; this straddling is where the name *Cowboy Rescue* comes from.

Step 3: Scramble Up the Kayak

From the back deck, you need to scramble up the kayak as if shinnying up a tree until you

The "Scramble" or "Cowboy" Reentry:
Step 1: Climb onto the Back Deck—
Balance your weight evenly across the stern.

Step 2: Straddle the Kayak—
Keep your balance as you carefully swing a leg over the stern.

Step 3: Scramble Up the Kayak—
Keeping your feet in the water for stability and your weight low, slide toward the cockpit on your elbows and inner thighs.

Step 4: Drop Your Butt into the Seat—
With your paddle out, ready to brace, drop your butt down into the seat.

Step 5: Get Your Legs In—
Use a sculling brace on the right for support while your left foot enters the cockpit.

reach the cockpit. Keep your weight low and move slowly and smoothly, slothlike, throughout the entire rescue. Hold your paddle across the deck in front of you so you can use it to brace if you start to lose your balance. Keep your legs splayed and your feet in the water. We often see beginners tip back over at this point because they pull their feet out of the water and put them on the back deck to help push themselves toward the cockpit. Your feet in the water are the only things stabilizing you. Hold them out away from the boat like pontoons for better balance.

There are also several tricks to crawling up the boat. As you move, don't slither on your belly like a snake. Your PFD will only tend to snag on the deck rigging. Instead, prop yourself up on your elbows and forearms, still keeping your center of gravity low but lifting your torso free of the rigging. Rock your pelvis back underneath you to lift your lower stomach. Don't lie on your stomach like a surfer on a surfboard. The position you want, the cowboy, is more like that of a jockey astride a racehorse: your weight is low, but your points of contact are your elbows and inner thighs, not your chest and stomach. In this "jockey" position, scootch up your kayak toward the cockpit. You may need to reach down and pull your skirt up from between your legs to keep it from snagging. Some paddlers put the grab loop in their teeth to keep it out of the way.

When you reach the cockpit, be careful of your seat back. If you knock it onto your seat and then sit on it when you reenter the cockpit, the extra height you'll gain from sitting on the seat back in a swamped boat usually creates enough instability to capsize you again.

Keep scootching across the cockpit until your butt is over your seat, clear of the seat back. Don't stop too soon or you'll sit on the seat back, and don't be surprised at how far up your front deck your face has to be to get your butt clear of the seat back. This last part—moving over the cockpit—is usually the most difficult, because you're on the highest, widest part of the boat. Move to the next step as quickly and smoothly as possible.

Step 4: Drop Your Butt into the Seat

Once you are clear of the seat back, drop your butt into the kayak seat. This is the final crux move, because you will be momentarily off balance as you raise your upper body off the front deck. To avoid capsizing after all the hard work you've just done, use your paddle as a brace on your dominant side. Before making the final move, get your paddle out on the right (assuming that's your strong side) with the face of the blade flat, ready for a High Brace. In one smooth, quick motion, raise your upper body as you slide your butt down into the seat and lean slightly to the right to slap the water with a High Brace.

Step 5: Get Your Legs In

Continue with a Sculling Brace for support while you put one leg into the cockpit. It's usually easier to start with the leg opposite the brace—the left, in our example. Find the foot peg with your first leg so you begin to gain some control over the kayak, then put your other leg into the cockpit, find the foot peg, pump the water out of your boat, replace the skirt, and continue on your way. The trick is getting your legs into the cockpit without raising your center of gravity back up onto the deck. Although tucking your legs in is definitely easier for paddlers with short legs (and large cockpits), Roger is well over 6 feet tall and scrambles with ease into most boats with standard-sized cockpits.

If your legs are too long or your cockpit too small, you can still paddle with a cockpit full of water and your legs hanging over the sides. Roger teaches this to tall students as a way to clear a surf zone or rock garden and move into calmer waters; there they can get help from a partner in stabilizing their kayaks while they get their legs inside.

Variations on the Scramble

A paddler with excellent balance can do Step 1 (climbing onto the kayak) right over the cockpit, then twist and drop her butt into the seat in one quick motion. We've heard this method referred to as the Taco, because you vault over the side and slide into the cockpit like stuffing meat into a taco shell. We have also seen the Scramble done like a Paddlefloat Reentry, with the paddler lying facedown on the back deck and corkscrewing into the cockpit feet-first, but we find this method much less stable, especially in rough water.

One of Roger's favorite variations is to combine the self-draining Bow Lift Fancy Flip, described in Chapter 5, with a quick Scramble. With this combination, you can be back in a relatively dry boat that needs little or no pumping within a matter of seconds, making it even faster than a Reenter and Roll (below), which fills the boat and requires lots of pumping. Roger's best practice time in rough-water conditions (8-foot ocean swells and chop with 30-knot winds), from capsize to a dry boat with the skirt on, ready to paddle, is well under a minute.

Scramble Practice Tips

Work backward through the steps in calm, shallow water. First practice the crux move of Step 4. Start by standing astride your cockpit in shin-deep water and dropping your butt smoothly and quickly into the seat. Once this feels balanced, try scrambling from just behind the cockpit, pushing off the ground for balance only if you need to. Gradually move into thigh-deep water, and try scrambling all the way from behind the back hatch, until you can complete the Scramble without pushing off the bottom. To practice Step 1 (getting on the back deck), move to waist-deep water and practice lying across the back deck and spinning to straddle the kayak. Then try it in chest-deep water. Work on it until you can complete the entire rescue without touching the bottom.

Quick as it is, the Scramble Rescue isn't easy and it's not for everyone. It requires good balance and lots of practice, especially to get it to work in rough water. In kayaks with small cockpits, it may be impossible to get your legs into the boat without help from a partner. Despite these challenges, the Scramble is still among our favorites and well worth spending time to develop. Roger has seen intermediate students use the Scramble in the middle of a wide surf zone to avoid the long swims that others were taking. Even if you are not able to make it work for you in real-life conditions, practicing it can help improve your overall comfort and balance in a kayak, especially for doing other rescues such as the Paddlefloat Reentry.

■ Reenter and Roll

The Reenter and Roll is potentially the fastest solo reentry in this book. Where the Reenter and Roll really comes into its own, however, is in rough seas, because it skips the vulnerable part of both the Paddlefloat Reentry and the Scramble—the point at which you climb on top of your kayak and try to balance. Still, it's a difficult rescue for some paddlers for fathom. Essentially it is an Eskimo Roll performed after exiting the kayak. You climb back into the upside-down cockpit underwater (this is the part that throws people), and then use the paddle to roll yourself back upright. This maneuver can be greatly facilitated by using a paddlefloat, although this sacrifices much of its speed. Either with or without a paddlefloat attached, some Eskimo Roll training is implied, so we generally consider this to be among the more advanced rescues. A small percentage of beginners do, however, find it easier to perform a paddlefloat Reenter and Roll than a standard Paddlefloat Rescue.

Step by Step
Reenter and Roll Using a Paddlefloat

Step 1: Reenter the Inverted Kayak

After attaching and inflating your paddlefloat as described earlier for the Paddlefloat rescue, face toward the bow while floating next to your capsized kayak and holding on to it with your near hand. If your braces or rolls are stronger on your right side, start on that side of the boat, so you'll be using your left hand to hold on to your kayak.

To keep track of your paddle, you can set it across the hull, perpendicular to the boat, with the paddlefloat resting on the water on your side, so it is already set up in a roll position. Alternately, some paddlers prefer to hold the paddle in the same hand as the kayak, parallel to it. When using this method, the blade that has the paddlefloat attached needs to be *toward* the bow.

Next, while floating on your back, start working your feet into the cockpit toward your foot braces. Try to get your legs as far into the kayak as possible; tilting the kayak on edge toward you will help.

Now for the hard part. Take a big breath, duck your head underwater, reach for the far side of your coaming with your right hand, and use your hands on either side of the cockpit to pull your butt up into the seat as if you were pulling on a tight pair of pants—only completely inverted, with the top of your head pointing to the bottom of the sea. Got that? While still holding your breath, find your foot braces with your feet and brace your knees firmly against the inside of the cockpit.

As an option, some paddlers prefer to somersault into their kayaks. To do this, start by facing toward the back of your kayak, and then reach across to grab the far side of the coaming with your right hand. Now, grabbing both sides of the cockpit, duck under and somersault your legs into the cockpit and your butt into the seat. It's not an easy move while wearing a PFD.

Step 2: Set Up to Roll

Braced upside down in your kayak, reach back up and grab your paddle shaft on the float side. If you didn't already set up your paddle perpendicularly in Step 1, you'll need to do so now: Sweep your right paddle blade (the one with the paddlefloat attached) out to the side of your kayak, just as you would for an Eskimo Roll.

Step 3: Roll

Once your paddle is in position, use it to roll yourself upright. Remember to use a good hip snap, bringing your head up last as described in the Eskimo Bow Rescue (below). Then get to work pumping out all that water that got scooped in with you when you rolled up.

Reenter and Roll Using a Paddlefloat:
Step 1: Reenter the Inverted Kayak—
Get back in by sliding your legs into the cockpit with your paddle held perpendicular.

Step 2: Set Up to Roll—
Prepare to roll by using your right hand under water to pull the kayak firmly into place around your hips and knees.

Step 3: Roll—
Roll back up using the paddlefloat for support.

Another version of this reentry is to Reenter and Roll without using the paddlefloat. This is obviously quicker, because it skips the step of attaching and inflating the paddlefloat.

Another version, which can be used with or without a paddlefloat, involves taking the time to reattach your skirt while holding your breath upside down. This is a challenging maneuver, but it will somewhat limit the large volume of water that typically gets scooped into your cockpit during this rescue.

One advantage of the Reenter and Roll without using a paddlefloat is that it's fast, taking only a matter of seconds, less than half the time usually needed for even the quickest Scramble Rescue. The big disadvantage is the prodigious amount of water that tends to reenter the cockpit with you from rolling up with your extra weight in the boat. Personally, we have found that any time saved by performing a Reenter and Roll instead of a Scramble was lost while pumping. The Reenter and Roll, however, is easier for some people than a Scramble, especially in rough seas or if paddling a kayak with a small cockpit that can't be scrambled. Again, though, this assumes that the paddler has the degree of skill necessary to perform an Eskimo Roll in the first place.

Using a paddlefloat to assist this rescue will make it much more accessible to lesser-skilled kayakers, but then the time required lengthens considerably. The Reenter and Roll with a paddlefloat is only slightly faster than a standard Paddlefloat Rescue, and, again, you'll end up having to pump a lot more water, so it will be slower in the long run. Also, we have found that a majority of beginners find this rescue as confusing as tax forms, so we usually wait to introduce it at more advanced levels. Even many advanced students seem to become disoriented when trying to reenter their kayaks by twisting around upside down underwater. However, for those few twisted beginners who actually find it easier than a standard Paddlefloat Rescue, we offer it as an alternative. The most useful application of a paddlefloat Reenter and Roll, though, will probably be as a backup to the standard Paddlefloat Rescue for

REAL LIFE RESCUES

Ride'em, Cowboy

Despite the gale warning on the marine weather radio this stormy November morning—or rather because of it—I find myself in my kayak, squinting into the rain and wind of a typical Pacific storm front. In the shelter of the Princeton Harbor jetties, my kayak chatters like an old truck on a bad washboard road into little more than a foot of wind chop. But from behind the jetty's gray stone walls, great spumes of spray reveal the true story. I pause in the lee of the jetty at the harbor mouth and look beyond at the unchecked sea. A stampede of 8-foot swells rumbles past, the surface whipped into a frenzy of wind waves and steep, breaking seas. I take a deep breath and spur the boat forward into the fray.

The sudden rush of wind that hits me is quickly dampened as I drop into the trough of an approaching swell. As the kayak climbs the face and the bow pierces its breaking crest, the wind returns, spattering me with a mixture of wave spray and rain. At the summit I catch a glimpse of turbid, slate-gray water, crumpled into irregular lumps like the hood of a wrecked car and mottled with sprays of white. I plunge into the following trough, bracing as much as paddling, making almost no headway.

After several minutes of hard paddling, I am well clear of the jetty. Looking around to get my bearings, I lean far to one side and capsize. Words from the safety saying I've repeated countless times to students echo back at me: "Don't paddle in water rougher than you've practiced rescues in." So instead of setting up for an Eskimo Roll, I pop my skirt and slide myself out of the warm, dark cockpit and into cold, dark water.

Buffeted by sloshing seas, I cling tightly to my kayak and paddle as I make my way hurriedly to the front of the boat, knowing that within minutes the wind and waves will wash me back into the jetty. I grab hold of the bow and time the swells. As I bob to the crest, I give a hard scissors kick with my legs and punch the bow skyward with my outstretched right arm. As the stern drops into the trough, most of the water in the cockpit drains to the aft bulkhead and dumps back into the sea; then with one quick motion, I spin the kayak back upright just before it drops back onto the water.

I scramble across the stern and straddle it like a cowboy on a bronco. I use my paddle to brace. Keeping my weight low, I slither up the kayak on my stomach like a child shinnying up a tree. When my face is even with the front-deck bungees and my butt is hovering over the cockpit, I wait to let a wave crest splash past, then quickly drop my butt into the seat, slapping a High Brace on the right, my strong side, for extra stability. I scull for support as another wave passes by. I lift my right leg into the cockpit and find the foot brace with my toes. In the lull of the next trough, I bring my left foot in.

I've drifted sideways to the swell by now, so I spin my bow back to face the waves before attempting to reseal the skirt, a tricky maneuver in rough seas. I let a crest pass, set the paddle across my lap, attach the skirt in back, grab the paddle and brace against the next swell, set the paddle down, finish attaching the skirt in front, grab the paddle, and brace again. Waves have sloshed a few inches of water back into the cockpit, but not so much that the kayak has become unstable. Skirt back in place, I turn and begin paddling back toward the harbor mouth, less than a minute from the time of capsize. Surging forward on the following seas with the wind behind me now, I make good time and slip back into the lee of the break wall and stop to catch my breath. Not exactly a real-life rescue, perhaps, but about as real as practice can get.

Roger

intermediate paddlers who are having trouble climbing onto their kayaks and balancing in very choppy seas.

One other application for this rescue deserves mention. By practicing only the final step—rolling up with the float attached—*with the skirt attached so you don't scoop water*, aspiring rollers can practice the movements involved in an Eskimo Roll while enjoying the extra support offered by the paddlefloat.

■ The Eskimo Bow Rescue

Next to the Eskimo Roll, the Bow Rescue is the quickest way to recover from a capsize, requiring only a few seconds and a handy partner nearby. It's so quick because it's not really a "reentry": You never actually leave your kayak. Instead of wet exiting after a capsize, you hold your breath for as long as possible (ten or twenty seconds is usually enough time) and wait upside down for your partner to paddle close enough for you to reach up, grab her bow, and use it to lever yourself back upright. When you're right-side up again, you're still seated in your kayak, skirt on, ready to paddle. One major drawback of the Bow Rescue is that it relies entirely on a quick response from a paddling partner. It also requires that the capsized paddler keep a cool head, summoning the patience and faith of a saint while breathlessly awaiting salvation.

Bow Rescues were originally developed by traditional kayak hunters, who didn't wet exit after capsizing because the equipment and skills they developed were based on the assumption that the kayak was part of the body when on the water and not removable. Often their skirts were sewn into the cockpit coaming, so they couldn't remove them in a hurry if they wanted to; their kayaks also had no flotation, nor did they wear clothing designed for swimming, so the ice-cold Arctic waters they paddled would kill a swimmer in minutes.

While Bow Rescues have worked in real-life capsizes, they enjoy a much broader application for modern-day paddlers in practice situations. Beginning paddlers can use the first part of the Bow Rescue progression described in Practicing the Eskimo Bow Rescue, below, to work on an

effective hip snap used in bracing and rolling. Intermediate paddlers will find that a Bow Rescue works very well as a way to practice actual bracing or rolling in deep water: With a partner ready nearby, you can avoid a wet exit if a brace or roll fails, simply by reaching up and righting yourself off her bow. More advanced paddlers can and do use the Bow Rescue as a viable alternative to a wet exit or Eskimo Roll.

Step by Step

Eskimo Bow Rescue

Step 1: Signal for Assistance

Whether you've capsized while practicing rolls with a partner nearby to spot you or you find yourself flipped for real, the first step is to signal for help. Do this by banging on your hull several times and waving your hands alongside your boat. Try to relax as best as you can given the situation. Panic burns oxygen. If you can calm yourself and hang out for a few seconds, you increase your odds of receiving a rescue that is much quicker, drier, warmer, and safer than if you wet exit your

Eskimo Bow Rescue: Step 1: Signal for Assistance—Remember to hold your hands out away from your hull to avoid getting them pinned by the bow of the rescue boat.

kayak. If you can keep your wits about you while upside down underwater, try to "chicken wing" your paddle between your arm and your body so you don't lose track of it.

It's very important to maintain a safe hand position. While awaiting rescue, don't leave your hands flat against your hull, where they can be crushed by an incoming bow. Instead, turn your hands sideways, pinkies out, presenting a much narrower profile. Hold your hands as far away from your kayak as possible.

In case your rescuer has bad aim, you will increase the likelihood of contacting the rescue bow if you wave your hands in as wide an arc as possible, and if you remember to tuck forward against your front deck so you will be able to get your hands higher out of the water. Also, move your hands slowly, or you might accidentally knock the bow away with frantic waving.

For the rescuer, speed is one of the key elements of an effective Eskimo Bow Rescue. Realize that the capsized paddler does not enjoy the same leisurely time frame as you in his anaerobic reality, so don't dally. On the other hand, you don't want to bomb in at ramming speed. You'll need to approach quickly, but *under control*. When you get close, use rudder strokes to slow down and to aim your bow

more precisely. Try to place your bow forward of the capsized kayak's cockpit, where it will be easier for the inverted paddler to grab. When you practice this, learn to *anticipate*. Have your paddle ready and start to move forward when the person you are spotting capsizes, so by the time he starts slapping his hull, you are already on your way.

In choppy conditions it can be difficult to place your bow in the hand of the capsized paddler. Instead of a ninety-degree approach angle, we have found it more effective to approach the overturned kayak at an angle of about forty-five degrees. Whether approaching from the front or back, aim 2 or 3 feet from the waving hands. Gauge your speed to use momentum to slide your bow alongside the upturned hull and into the waiting grasp. For this rescue to work, getting into a perpendicular position is not required—putting your bow in your capsized partner's hand is.

Step 2: Grab the Rescue Bow and Roll Up

When you hear the sweet *thunk* of the rescue bow and feel it slide into your hand, take a moment to orient yourself. If you've grabbed the bow behind your head, you'll need to move it in front of you and adjust your grasp before trying to roll up. Use a good hip snap, bringing your head

Rescue Boat Making Contact—
The rescuer needs to approach quickly but in control.

Step 2: Grab the Rescue Bow and Roll Up—
Use a hip snap and bring your head up last.

up last, and find your paddle quickly before it floats away.

Practicing the Eskimo Bow Rescue

Like the Eskimo Roll, the Bow Rescue is a fairly complicated procedure that is much easier to learn in steps. We've divided these steps into exercises for beginners and those for intermediate or advanced paddlers, so that each can progress at whatever pace seems comfortable.

Step by Step

Eskimo Bow Rescue
Exercises for Beginners

Step 1: Home Position

With your partner's bow at your hip forming a T-shape on your strong side (we'll describe this with your partner's bow on the right for consistency of directions), grab her bow with your right hand and rock your boat side to side like a hula dancer. This exercise will be easier if your kayak fits snugly, so you might want to adjust your foot braces a notch or two tighter than you do when touring.

Next grab your partner's bow with both hands. To free your hands, give your paddle to your partner, who can nest it together with her own. Lean your boat toward your partner, lifting your left knee. Keep leaning until you can rest your cheek against her bow and your kayak is vertical on its right side. Continue to lift your left knee and rock your left ear against your shoulder, stretching out the right side of your torso and scrunching up the left to form a C-shape with your body. Try to rock the kayak past vertical and on top of you until as much hull as possible is out of the water. This is what we call home position; get comfortable with it, because you'll be returning home often.

Step 2: Rock Up

Without removing your cheek from your hands, try to rock your body into a C-position on

Eskimo Bow Rescue Exercises for Beginners: Step 1: Home Position—
Get in the home position for practicing Eskimo Bow Rescues.

Step 2: Rock Up—
Rock up, rolling your boat underneath you and bringing your head up last.

the opposite (right) side. To do this, raise your right knee and drop your right ear to your right shoulder. With your head still resting on the bow of your partner's boat, you are trying to get the boat back underneath you with the hull as flat on the water as possi-ble. This C to C motion of your body, known as a hip snap, is a technique that is not only essential to this rescue but also the cornerstone of good bracing and Eskimo Rolls. So don't rush through this part of the exercise. Practice hip snaps back and forth from C to C several times without lifting your head from your partner's bow.

Now you are ready to rock up. Return to home with a strong C-bend to the left. Rock your boat crisply beneath you as you hip snap into a C-bend on the right, and allow your momentum to pull you back upright over your boat, pushing slightly off the bow with your hands. Note that your boat should come up first and that your head should come up last, with your ear against your right shoulder. Instead of *pushing* yourself up over your kayak with your hands, the idea is to *pull* your boat underneath you with your knees. (To get a feel for how much more effort is needed with poor technique, try this again leading with your head raised against your left shoulder and pushing with your hands.)

Try rocking up several times until it feels easy. From a standpoint of technique, you've completed the hardest part of this rescue. The rest of it is mostly in your head—developing the composure to think with your head upside down underwater.

Step 3: Dunk Your Head

Return home. Let your cheek slide off your hands and lower your face into the water. Then return home and rock up. To keep water out of your nose, make a "scrunchy face" while blowing air bubbles slowly out your nose, or buy some nose clips from a kayak shop. In cold water you might also try donning a hood.

Mentally this head dunking can be the hardest part for some paddlers. But don't let that stop you. It's only water. Developing the ability to relax underwater is key to learning both this rescue

and the Eskimo Roll. Practice dunking your head deeper in the water with each attempt and increasing the amount of time you spend hanging out underwater. See if you can count to three before rocking back up. Then try again, counting to five. With subsequent practice sessions, see if you can hold your breath for ten or twenty seconds or longer.

As you progress, don't let your technique get sloppy: Remember to return home before rocking your head up last, with your ear against your shoulder. Your partner should remember that your technique is likely to deteriorate after you dunk your head. Her job is to keep an eye on this and to keep reminding you to bring your head up *last*.

The next step in the head-dunking progression is to let go with one hand and allow the kayak to roll completely upside down, flat on the water. To do this, you'll need to let go momentarily with your right hand when you dunk your head. Count to three, then reach up, grab the bow again with your right hand, and return home. Catch your breath. Now try it again, but this time when you let go, reach across to the far side and smack your hull three times with your right hand before returning home. In real life smacking the hull is used to signal your paddling partners that you need a Bow Rescue.

Next try letting go and pounding the hull with both hands before you relocate the bow and rock yourself back up. Now you are ready to try it for real. Push your partner's boat back a couple of feet, take a big breath, and capsize. To keep track of your paddle, cradle it in your armpit chicken-wing style when you dump.

Bang on your boat to signal your partner, and wave your hands slowly alongside your boat—remembering the importance of safe hand position described above—until you feel her bow. Grab it, go home, and rock up, just like you've been doing. Don't allow the fact that you let go to psych you out. When you are up, get into the habit of finding your paddle right away. In rough seas you won't have much time before it washes away.

REAL LIFE RESCUES

Counting in Dog Years—
Tale of a Rock Garden Bow Rescue

I have been on the rescuing end of Bow Rescues on several real-life occasions, using my bow to salvage paddling partners in rock gardens, sea caves, and open water. In most of these scenarios, the capsized paddlers were trying to Eskimo Roll, and were getting enough air on each unsuccessful attempt to give me time to paddle over and proffer my bow. Once, however, the tables were turned.

A few years back I was teaching an advanced rock garden class on the northern California coast. I was demonstrating to the students how to run chutes, picking progressively more difficult lines to show a range of possibilities. One chute was very narrow, about an arm's span wide, several boat lengths long, and shallow. It only had enough water to float a kayak, in fact, when a large wave poured through. The swell was running 4 to 6 feet, and I lined up just outside the gap and waited as a set approached. I took off a little late on the first wave and had only surfed three-quarters of the way through the chute when the water dropped out from under me. My kayak was left high and dry at an angle across the gap, balanced precariously on the rocks by its bow and stern with about a 4-foot drop into a barnacle-encrusted crevice below me.

My bow had gotten wedged between some rocks, and I tried to free it as the next wave poured through and partially floated my boat. As the second wave receded, my kayak started to tip over. I didn't want to be wedged upside down in the crevice, so I instinctively thrust out my hands, one against each wall, to balance myself. While this quick reaction did prevent a capsize, I was unable to maintain hold of my paddle and brace on the rocks at the same time. I watched with a sinking feeling as my paddle floated away with the receding wave. The last wave of the set was the biggest and flushed me the rest of the way through the chute, but without a paddle, I was unable to maintain my balance in the turbulent waters and capsized.

I knew my co-instructor and good paddling buddy, Tom, was on the ocean side of the chute, narrating the play-by-play for the students. I also knew he would have to take the long way around the chute to get to me, since there were no more waves at the moment. I slapped my hull to let him know I'd like a Bow Rescue.

And I waited.

I can be extremely stubborn when it comes to wet exiting. I hate to jump out of a perfectly dry boat if there is anything I can do to avoid it. Realizing Tom wouldn't be arriving anytime soon, I tried a Hand Roll (an Eskimo Roll using only your hands). Although I'm usually successful with this technique in a river kayak and certain sea kayaks, I had experienced limited success with it in the particular sea kayak I was paddling that day. I came up far enough to get a gulp of air, but that was it. Instead of wasting more breath on failed Hand Roll attempts, I dog-paddled my face to the surface just enough to breathe. I would tire eventually and have to wet exit, but for the time being I had air. Had I been carrying my own spare paddle (Tom had it), I could have pulled it out from the bungees and used it to roll up with. Since that day I always make it a point to carry a spare paddle on my boat.

Time slows, I'd told my students many times, when you are awaiting a Bow Rescue. After what seemed like minutes, I saw Tom's yellow bow approaching from the south. I took one last big gulp of air, and dropped back under the water, raising my hands and waving them alongside my boat. I heard the comforting *thunk* of his kayak knocking into mine and felt the solid curve of his bow slip into my waiting hand. All in all he estimated it took him about forty-five seconds to reach me, which is about three minutes in dog years, the time frame also used by capsized kayakers.

Roger

Practicing Intermediate and Advanced Skills

With your partner lined up in a T-position as nearby as possible without getting in the way, test your braces, tipping over farther each time until you finally capsize. Then slap your hull, wave your hands, grab your partner's bow, and roll yourself back up. You can also practice Eskimo Rolls this way; just make sure to save enough breath after your final attempt to roll so you'll have enough air for a Bow Rescue. We usually wear helmets when practicing Bow Rescues.

In an actual capsize there is no telling from which direction the rescue boat may come. To prepare for this, more advanced paddlers can practice getting comfortable grabbing the bow from either side and at different approach angles.

A technique you can use to buy time while waiting for a Bow Rescue to arrive is to dog-paddle up for a breath of air. Be careful, however, that you don't end up with a kayak facial by sticking your head up at the wrong time. If you lose your paddle in a capsize, you can even use this technique to swim after your paddle while still in your kayak, and then use the paddle to Eskimo Roll.

A variation on the Eskimo Bow Rescue is for the rescuer to grab the bow of the capsized kayak and use it as a pivot point to swing her bow around precisely into the hands of the capsized paddler. What this version gains in precision, however, it loses in speed, taking several extra seconds—which can seem like forever to a submerged paddler.

Another variation is for the rescuer to offer a paddle instead of a bow to the capsized paddler. In this Paddle Bridge method, the rescuer comes up parallel to the capsized boat and lays her paddle across both boats, forming a stable bridge. She then grabs the capsized paddler's hand and places it on the paddle shaft, which the capsized paddler uses to roll up. Again, the precision of this version adds time, and in rough seas, the kayaks run the risk of bashing together and smashing the hands or head of the capsized paddler.

Bow Rescues are extremely useful for beginner and intermediate paddlers to practice bracing and rolling skills in deep water, and for learning to relax when upside down underwater. However, we have heard some paddlers claim that Bow Rescues are *only* good in practice situations. Thousands of traditional paddlers would disagree. And so would we. We have used this rescue successfully with experienced paddlers—especially those with some Eskimo Roll training—in actual rough-water capsizes, provided they were able to keep a calm head and hold their breath, and that they had reliable partners nearby who could get to them before their air ran out.

We do agree that the application of the Bow Rescue in real-life capsizes is typically limited to fairly advanced paddlers with strong skills and good teamwork. Also, capsized paddlers who don't remember to hold their hands in the safe position run the risk of getting their fingers smashed by the incoming bow. But for kayakers willing to stay in their boats for the seeming eternity it takes for a rescue bow to arrive, the Eskimo Bow Rescue can—and has—worked in a variety of real-life rescues.

■ Eskimo Rolls: The Ultimate Self-Rescue

The Eskimo Roll is, of course, the fastest, most efficient way to recover from a capsize, and it has numerous advantages over all other methods of capsize recovery. It takes only seconds to complete. It does not rely on another paddler. You don't wet exit your kayak, so you stay drier and warmer. It can be performed in the roughest of conditions. Heck, it even looks cool. A solid roll can give you the confidence to experiment with new skills and challenging conditions in which capsize is likely. Whether you are just perfecting leaned turns and bracing skills on flat water or you are playing in the surf, tide rips, or rock gardens, a roll allows you to push the envelope without having to swim. The obvious downside is that it can be quite challenging for some paddlers to learn and even more difficult to master to the point where it will actually work in real-life "combat" situations when you need it.

A roll is essentially an extreme form of a

High Brace in which you use your paddle as a lever to pry yourself from completely upside down back to upright, after a capsize. The original Eskimo paddlers were not oriented toward wet exiting into Arctic waters. They had no PFDs, no wet suits or dry suits, and their sprayskirts (or anoraks) were sometimes sewn onto their cockpits. A wet exit was not an option, so after a capsize they were faced with a roll-or-die situation if no partner was nearby to offer a Bow Rescue.

Paddling in this reality, the original kayak hunters developed literally dozens of rolls—about as many types of rolls as they had words for snow. Many were developed in response to specific hunting accidents or extreme sea conditions. There were one-armed rolls to deal with situations in which an arm was injured or tangled in the harpoon line; ways to roll up using the hands, the hunter's atlatl (harpoon-throwing stick), or seal-bladder float in case the paddle was lost; and "storm" rolls for gnarly weather. While the annual Greenland National Kayak Championships recognize some thirty distinct rolls, we want to focus on the two or three used most commonly by the majority of modern-day recreational paddlers.

These days most sea kayakers learn either a Sweep Roll or a C to C Roll or some blend of the two. We like to teach our students a Sweep to C hybrid that blends the stronger parts of each, and then let each student gravitate toward one end of the spectrum or the other, depending on factors such as body type, flexibility, kind of kayak, and personal preference. Some paddlers just seem to have an easier time with one style.

Our intention is not to teach rolling from a book. It's nearly impossible, although we have heard of a few rare exceptions—students who have actually learned just from reading books like *The Bombproof Roll and Beyond* by Paul Dutky or *Eskimo Rolling* by Derek Hutchinson. The rest of us mere mortals need to take a class from a competent instructor. What we want is for you to go to that class already armed with an understanding of the Eskimo Roll. We also want to introduce some hip snap drills that you can practice on your own or with a friend in shallow water, so you'll have some of the basic concepts down.

Sweep Roll

Sometimes also called the Screw Roll or Back Deck Roll, this roll involves sweeping the paddle out at an arc to the side with the paddle face flat to the surface of the water. As the paddle meets the resistance of the water, your lower body will begin to boost the kayak back over onto its hull. You'll need to lay your head back and turn it to focus your line of sight on the paddle blade that is continuing to move across the surface of the water and behind you.

Step by Step
Sweep Roll

Step 1: Setup

Most right-handed people will place the paddle parallel to the left side of the kayak, tucking to get their right-hand blade as far forward and as close to the surface of the water as possible.

Optionally, some paddlers like to set up using an extended-paddle or Pawlata position. Named for the paddler who in 1927 became the first person in Europe to perform an Eskimo Roll, this setup involves sliding your offside (left) hand all the way to the end of the paddle blade in order to gain more leverage.

Step 2: Sweep

Push your right hand as far up and to your left as possible. Keep your left hand on your kayak near your left hip as a pivot. Sweep the right-hand paddle blade across the surface in an arc away from the bow.

Step 3: Hip Snap

As the paddle approaches the midpoint of its arc, your lower body needs to start pulling the kayak around to your right side. Think of your knees and hips drawing the kayak back under your head. Your right thigh will need to contract toward your right ribs, your left leg relaxing or extending, feet firm on the foot braces.

Step 4: Complete the Sweep and Roll

Lay your upper body back, then look down

Sweep Roll: Step 1: Setup—
Set up by bringing your paddle alongside your kayak, right wrist near left knee (if rolling on the right).

Step 2: Sweep—
Sweep your right blade out in an arc along the surface.

Steps 3 and 4: Hip Snap and Complete the Sweep and Roll—
Use your lower body to pull the kayak under you. Complete the sweep and roll up, keeping your head down and your eyes focussed toward the paddle blade.

the line of your paddle to the right-hand blade, which is now behind you on your right. The other side of the paddle should be near your left elbow and no higher than your left shoulder.

The common tendency is to focus on the role of the paddle through the roll, but what your torso and head do is more important. In the Sweep Roll you need first to tuck forward and toward your pivot hand as much as possible. Your torso will unwind from forward-left to back-right in a counterclockwise direction. Your head must stay down to the right at the finish; lying as far back as possible will help. Think of a pole vaulter, who sets the pole then extends her legs from a tucked position up and over the bar ahead of her upper body. This kind of roll requires a good contact with the paddle and the surface of the water.

C to C Roll

In this roll your torso will not travel an arc but simply crunch up on one side and then crunch up over to the opposite side. The paddle goes directly to ninety degrees with the hull of the kayak, but above the surface of the water. Then the paddle is used in the same motion as in the High Brace, meeting the resistance of the water while your hip brings the kayak back under your head.

C to C Roll: Step 1: Setup—
Set up the same as in the Sweep Roll. Bring your paddle alongside your kayak, right wrist near left knee.

Step 2: Sweep—
Sweep the paddle out 90 degrees from your kayak, with the blade flat on the surface of the boat and your left hand reaching as far over the hull as possible. Push your head left toward your hip, coiling your body into a C.

Step by Step
C to C Roll

Step 1: Setup

The setup is the same as for the Sweep Roll, above.

Step 2: Sweep

The paddle goes to ninety degrees without touching the water surface, if possible. This time your left hand is also a pivot, but the hand and forearm will be pushed as far over the bottom side of your kayak to your left as possible. Really flexible people can get their right hand next to the left side of their kayak while the paddle is not

Step 3: Hip Snap—
Hip snap vigorously, rolling the kayak under you and bringing your head up last.

parallel but at a right angle to the hull and above and flat to the surface of the water. Push your head left and as close to your hip as possible, coiling your body sideways into a C-shape.

Step 3: Hip Snap

Plant your paddle flat on the surface and uncoil your body into a C-shape on the opposite side: Snap your hip and right thigh, quickly forcing your head toward your right hip, over your right ribs while you bring the kayak back underneath you. Resist the temptation to drive your left hand up, because that pushes the paddle down and doesn't give the same quality of lift.

The C to C requires less attention to the paddle and more to the snap of the body. It works well for people who can't lean back or who have trouble keeping the paddle blade just along the surface of the water.

Roll Practice Tips

For all kinds of rolls, it is helpful to have nose clips or a scuba mask for practice. Start with working on your hip snaps as described in

Chapter 3 for bracing and in this chapter for the Bow Rescue. You can also practice using a paddlefloat on the right-hand blade of the paddle to practice hip snaps and to feel the stretch required to reach the surface of the water. To avoid muscling your way up off the paddlefloat, gradually deflate the float so that it will sink if you don't finesse your way up.

If you have a willing companion, ask him to work with you in shallow water. He can hold the right-hand blade of your paddle while you practice the hip snap, getting your kayak all the way over on top of you while your face stays just above water. In this position you can rock the kayak back and forth over you while your friend supports the paddle. Be sure to practice dropping your head to the right shoulder as you come up; the head counterbalances the snap of the hip. Eventually your assistant can guide the paddle from the setup position through the arc or to the hip snap position. When you are ready to try your roll in deep water, have a watchful friend stand by, ready to offer his bow for the Eskimo Bow Rescue, described earlier in this chapter, while you practice your first few.

After you've had some roll training and want to practice on your own, try a shallow, sandy beach in about 3 feet of water. You want only enough depth to tip over without hitting your head; it should still be shallow enough that you can push yourself back up off the bottom (a Pole Roll) if you need to. If you are not having success, we recommend seeking professional instruction to avoid picking up bad habits. As counterintuitive as most rolls are to start with, and as frustrating as they can be to learn, they are a wonderful alternative to any form of reentry.

> **Reminders: Tips for Learning to Roll**
>
> 1. **Don't Rush Your Roll:** Keep your motions slow, smooth, and deliberate. The paddle floats, so skim it across the surface, don't pull it down.
> 2. **Boat First:** Use your lower body to initiate the kayak's roll through knee and hip contact.
> 3. **Head Last:** Keep your head down, relax your neck or snap your head down to your shoulder.

■ Chapter 7

Rescues for Special Circumstances

■ Tired Paddlers

■ Incapacitated Paddlers

■ Flotation Problems

■ Loaded Kayaks

■ Doubles & Sit-on-Tops

■ Surf & Rough Water

This chapter deals with strategies for handling situations that are beyond the norm—those that involve tired or incapacitated swimmers, rough seas, sinking boats, and any number of complications. We laughed when we wrote that last sentence because our *normal* rescue scenarios are often "beyond the norm." You may think that some of these rescues seem to stretch the "what if" idea a bit thin, but a lot of weird stuff happens out on the water.

When we practiced rescues like the Cleopatra's Needle for the first time, we did so for fun, thinking, *yeah, sure, like a hatch cover is ever actually going to come off on the water*. But when it happened for the first time, after a breaking wave in the surf zone removed a poorly designed cover, we were only momentarily shocked. Not only were we dealing with a flooded hatch and vertical kayak, but we were doing so between breaking waves, too. So it goes.

Hopefully you'll never have to deal with flooded hatches, unconscious swimmers, or loaded doubles. On the other hand, if you familiarize yourself with these rescues, you'll be better able to deal with whatever happens—like maybe having to tow an unconscious swimmer to his loaded double with a blown hatch cover. In a sea cave, of course. Knock on wood and have fun practicing.

■ Sling Rescues for Tired Paddlers

Sling Rescues require a loop of line that is sometimes called a stirrup because a swimmer can step into it to get back onto her kayak, much the way a rider uses a stirrup to mount a horse. Using a sling is indicated when a swimmer is too tired or weak to pull herself out of the water and onto the kayak to start a rescue. A sling can be used for a self-rescue with a paddlefloat or in any of a number of assisted rescues.

Paddlefloat with a Sling Rescue

This reentry is essentially the same as the basic Paddlefloat Self-Rescue described in Chapter 5, but the sling is used to help the swimmer use her leg strength to boost herself up onto her back deck. This is an especially good solo rescue for swimmers with small hands or too little energy to swim onto their back decks. It also works well for paddlers who have limited upper-body strength.

Paddlefloat with a Sling Rescue:
Step 2: Rig the Sling—
Put the loop around the paddle neck.

Step by Step

Paddlefloat with a Sling Rescue

Step 1: Secure the Paddlefloat

As with the basic Paddlefloat Self-Rescue, leave the kayak upside down, put one foot in it while you pull out the paddlefloat, put the float on the paddle, inflate it, take your foot out of the cockpit, and right the kayak.

Step 2: Rig the Sling

Hang on to the kayak with your hand or elbow in the cockpit. Slip the loop of line over the paddle blade that doesn't have the paddlefloat on

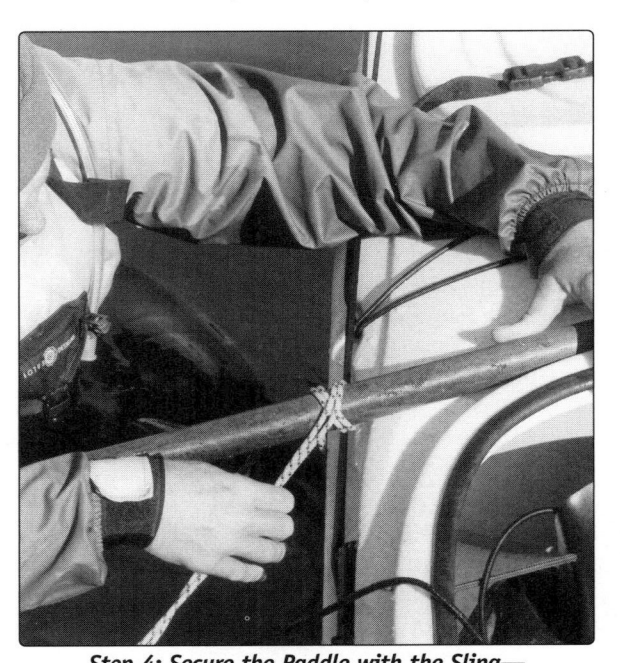

Step 4: Secure the Paddle with the Sling—
Run the first wrap between the loop and the kayak, then over itself as many times as necessary to adjust the length.

Step 5: Step onto the Sling—
Step up and lay your stomach across the back deck.

it so that the line hangs down from the neck of the paddle. Position yourself behind both your paddle and your cockpit. It doesn't matter which side of the kayak you are on, as long as you and the paddlefloat are on the same side.

Some paddlers rig their own kayaks with a permanent stirrup that is tied into the back-deck rigging and preadjusted to their leg length. The extra line can be wound up and stowed under the bungees and pulled out on either side after a capsize. This can save time for any paddlers who know they regularly need a sling.

Step 3: Orient the Paddle and Sling to the Kayak

Place the paddle at a right angle to the kayak, just as for a standard Paddlefloat Rescue, with the shaft just behind the cockpit next to the coaming and the paddlefloat on your side. Let the loop hang down from the neck of the paddle on the far side of the kayak and into the water.

Step 4: Secure the Paddle with the Sling and Adjust It for Length

While still holding on to the kayak, push it gently away from you and reach under the kayak

for the hanging loop. Pull the loop under the kayak and wrap it up over the paddle shaft. Next secure it by passing it between itself and the boat, and wrap it snugly over itself several times until the loop is the proper length: hanging down about a foot below your kayak or in front of your stomach.

Make sure the first overlap of the line around the paddle goes between the line and the kayak, instead of between the line and the paddlefloat. The idea is to keep the line from spiraling down the paddle shaft like the red line on an old-fashioned barber's pole. Some paddlers use a girth hitch or special knot to secure the sling into position. Just be sure that whatever you use, your choice is easy to release after you are in your seat facing away from your knots.

Step 5: Step onto the Sling

Depending on your flexibility, you may need the loop to hang down to your stomach or some-what deeper and closer to the knee end of your thigh. Ideally it will be high enough that when you step into it and extend your leg, your upper stomach will land on the back deck of your kayak with your navel about centered on the boat's midline. When you step into the sling, the toes that are toward the bow belong in the loop—that is, if you are on the right side of the kayak, you will put your right foot into the loop. Step up on the loop while pulling the kayak toward you and under your stomach.

To avoid having your legs float up under the kayak, a common problem for some paddlers, you'll need to get the foot that is in the loop directly below your torso. After your foot goes into the loop, pull yourself toward the loop so it passes straight down as you pull yourself onto the kayak. Some people squeeze the sling down between their thighs after their foot is in it; this helps them center their legs underneath them and puts them into a squatting position.

It also works well for short-legged people to position themselves in front of the paddle shaft next to the cockpit. If you are on the right side of the kayak, your left foot will go into the sling and the right one will go into the cockpit after you have your belly up on the paddle shaft and back deck of your kayak. This method makes it more difficult to extract your foot from the sling, because the foot in the cockpit can't help push the line away from the foot in the loop, which is the next step.

Step 6: Remove Your Foot from the Sling

Carefully release your foot from the loop or put both feet on the paddlefloat and use your left foot to push the loop off your right foot. Extracting the foot is the crux move. Some people have trouble with their cold feet sliding through the loop, or with maintaining just the right amount of tension on the line to hold it into place until they need to release it. Remember to move slowly and deliberately. If you can at least get yourself up and out of the water, you'll be more comfortable and at less risk than if you're immersed.

Step 7: Reenter the Cockpit

Once the sling is out of the way, resume the reentry—one leg at a time. Rotating on your stomach, slowly and smoothly move the first leg into the cockpit. Bring your hand out to the paddle shaft to bear weight on the shaft while you move your second leg into the cockpit. Remember to keep leaning onto the paddlefloat, keeping your weight low as you switch hands and corkscrew into the cockpit.

Step 8: Remove the Sling from the Paddle and Pump Out

Bring the paddle up and over your head while continuing to lean on the float, pull the loop off your paddle, and stow it. Longer slings will require a little unwrapping or some slow pulling while they unwind themselves; shorter loops will lift right up with the release of the one or two wraps they need to be secured. Put your paddle across your lap and lean on it for support as you pump your cockpit.

The sling is an extremely useful and inexpensive piece of gear to add to your bag of tricks. The Paddlefloat with a Sling Rescue requires some extra manipulation and care to avoid the pitfalls of tangling in a line. Practice with it will give you a powerful self-rescue to use if you are alone and having trouble getting onto your boat.

Assisted Rescue with a Sling

If you find a swimmer who is having trouble getting back onto her kayak, the simplest way to help her is to lean across her kayak, keeping one arm across to stabilize it, grasp her PFD shoulder with the other hand, and pull her up onto her back deck. But if you aren't able to yank her in, the sling will let her use her leg strength to step up and then lie on her kayak. This is a great assisted rescue to enable swimmers who just don't have the upper-body strength to *pull* themselves up but do have the lower-body strength to *push* themselves up onto their kayak. Our first choice would be to use the sling in conjunction with a T Rescue, but depending on the swimmer's response you may find one of the other assisted rescues (TX, Assisted T, or Reenter and Pump) to be more appropriate.

Step by Step

Assisted Rescue with a Sling

Step 1: Check In and Initiate a Rescue

Assess the situation and decide which type of assisted rescue to initiate.

Step 2: Rig the Sling

Finish the first part of the rescue and get the kayaks parallel, facing bow to stern and ready for stabilizing with both paddles across the cockpits. Now take the sling and feed it around the swimmer's cockpit coaming. The sling should sit in the groove just outside and below the bump that the sprayskirt fits around. It will need to be adjusted for length. Have the swimmer hold the line at the level she thinks will make a good step, usually 1 to 3 feet below the kayak. While she holds the line in place, tie a quick knot in the part of the loop that is nearest to you to adjust the loop to the size of step needed. Jan likes to use an over-hand knot, and Roger uses a slip knot; either way, make it something simple that can be readjusted in a hurry.

We see a lot of different ways to tie a sling in our instructor workshops and in magazines. One elaborate method in print involves tying both paddles *below* both kayaks with the sling; the swimmer then steps on the paddle blades. We definitely do not recommend this. A more popular method is to wrap the two paddles together on top of the kayaks and let the loop hang down from the paddles; this is effective but time consuming. Another style is to wrap the sling around your own coaming or around your torso, but this seems like an unnecessary risk to you. We like to keep it simple and quick, which is why we like the coaming method, and we find that putting the sling around the coaming of the swimmer's kayak works well. Some people find that putting the loop around the swimmer's cockpit twists the kayak out of the stabilizer's hands when the swimmer steps up. We haven't seen this happen yet, even with small rescuers stabilizing for extra-large swimmers, but maybe that's because we use an effective pit-to-pit stabilizing technique.

Assisted Rescue with a Sling: Step 2: Rig the Sling—
Rig the sling by wrapping the line around the groove below the cockpit coaming.

Step 4: Swimmer Steps Up—
The swimmer steps up and lays across the back deck.

Step 3: Stabilize

Hold both sides of the cockpit coaming as you would for any variation of an assisted rescue. Lie across the kayak just in front of the cockpit, arms over both paddles, in what we call the pit-to-pit position—your armpit to her cockpit.

Step 4: Swimmer Steps Up

If she is getting into her kayak from the right-hand side, she will use her right leg. As she looks at you, whichever leg is closer to the front of her kayak should initiate the step up. She needs to pull the line taunt, straight down from the kayak, with the ball of her foot on the line. She gets her body moving up and forward, at a slight angle toward the back deck, as she pulls on the far side (your side) of the back of her coaming. Although the sling's leverage point is directly to the side of the cockpit, she needs to lay her stomach and chest onto the back deck of her kayak so that eventually she can swing her legs into the cockpit. As soon as she can reach your kayak, she helps hold the two kayaks together.

Step 5: Remove Foot from the Sling

Getting the foot out of the sling is always a challenge, but using the around-the-cockpit method keeps the loop open. While the ex-swimmer is on her back deck and helping you hold the raft together, encourage her to catch her breath, and then to move slowly and deliberately to slip her foot free of the line.

Step 6: Reenter the Cockpit

This rescue finishes just as other assisted rescues do: The ex-swimmer puts her legs into her cockpit, moves her pelvic bones over her seat, twisting toward you, and corkscrews into the seat.

Step 7: Remove the Sling

Take the line off of the cockpit coaming and stow it. Help get the ex–swimmer's sprayskirt back on while you assess her condition to determine if she will need further stabilization or if she will be able to paddle to shore on her own.

Sling Tips

We each like to keep our sling handy in a PFD pocket. Jan uses 12 feet of ⅜-inch sinking line. Roger uses about 15 feet of ½-inch webbing that will float. Both styles hold a permanent knot well.

REAL LIFE RESCUES

T Rescue with a Sling—Under the Golden Gate

One day after landing for lunch at Kirby Cove, just outside (seaward of) the Golden Gate Bridge in San Francisco, we noticed that the tidal current appeared to be ebbing earlier than the tide book had predicted. Instead of a "slack" tide for our return beneath the Gate, we made slow headway into about a 2- to 3-knot ebb. Just after the paddlers in the lead made it around the tower where the current was most focused, one of the rear paddlers capsized, missed his roll, and wet exited right in front of me.

While Roger gathered the group just inside the bay, I started a T Rescue, dumping out the cockpit quickly, slapping the kayak back down onto the water, and stabilizing it. "Okay, you ready?" I asked, eager to get Frank back in his kayak and rejoin the rest of the group. I had noticed that the others had disappeared around the corner and out of sight, and that the current was sweeping the two of us toward the open sea, choppy water dancing all around us.

"Yeah, Jan," he said without much enthusiasm. "I think so."

When Frank tried to pull himself onto the back deck, the current swept his legs under his kayak, and he slid back into the water. And I started to worry. He was a large man, about 6 foot 4 and 240 pounds, and he looked tired after a long day of paddling—too tired, perhaps, to get onto his kayak without some help. I'm a fairly strong woman for my size, but at 5 foot 4 and 125 pounds, I began to fear that he might just be too big for me to yank in. I saw that just the effort of him tugging himself onto his back deck had swamped the kayak; if I were to let go with one hand to grab him, it might result in the kayak rolling and swamping further.

I encouraged him to kick his legs out behind him and try again. He kicked his feet hard, struggling to pull himself up. But even then he wasn't able to pull himself onto his deck. He slid back into the water, breathing hard. I realized that without some kind of help, he wouldn't be able to get out of the cold water that was quickly sapping his strength despite his wet suit.

"Catch your breath, Frank," I told him, trying hard to sound positive. "And we'll try again. Don't worry. We'll get it." But I wasn't so sure. I could see that we were quickly drifting, farther and farther from shore. Then I thought about the sling in my PFD pocket, and knew it was the next thing to try.

I quickly ran the sling around his cockpit and urged him to step onto it. He reached down and tucked his foot into the loop. Slowly he began to lean forward and pull himself up. Then, rising from the sea like Poseidon, he landed squarely onto the back deck. With the help of the sling he was able to get back into his cockpit without a problem. Still, even though he was out of the fire, so to speak, we were still in the frying pan. Now that he was in his kayak, its cockpit was totally swamped, and the combined weight of water and paddler was keeping the coaming just beneath the surface.

We held on to each other's cockpits while securing his skirt, but found that pumping was impossible with his skirt on. The only place that the pump could fit into his cockpit was directly between his knees, front and center. "Frank," I said, "you need a bigger boat." He grinned, "I know, I know. This kayak was fine in Florida where the water was flat, but we're a long way from Florida." I knew there was no way he could paddle the swamped kayak without capsizing, so I held on. I thought about my radio, knowing that the Coast Guard was nearby, but I felt that our situation had greatly improved with him back in his boat. I felt like a Band-Aid—our situation would not be completely healed by just holding on to each other, but temporarily, we were covered. We drifted farther out to sea, the water mellowing to mild rollers as we left the steep chop caused by the current meeting the bridge tower and the incoming swell.

Soon Roger emerged from around the tower along with another strong paddler. They quickly realized that the reentry was not going according to plan and that Frank and I needed some help. Roger and the other paddler hooked up tow ropes. While I continued to stabilize the swamped kayak, the two of them towed us back toward shore. I smiled to myself, thankful for the sling in my pocket and for the reliability of my paddling partners.

Jan

We recommend tying a water knot, a double fisherman's knot or a square knot. Most people paddling single sea kayaks find that a length of line of about 12 to 16 feet tied into a circle works well for them. Some people prefer ½–inch floating line, which is bulkier and more expensive but also holds a knot well without becoming permanent under a load. These bigger lines might not fit into a pocket; they may need to be carried in a PFD pouch, or you might have to make a special wrap to keep one handy in deck bungees. Your sling needs to be accessible but securely stowed so it won't deploy on its own or be swept away by rough seas.

We have experimented with using our tow ropes as slings and found the dual system to be a little too awkward. We have seen a couple of people with 20 to 25 feet of webbing tied into a stirrup. It seemed a little bulky for single kayaks, but they said that a long sling gave them more flexibility with doubles, and that the lengthy sling could work on single kayaks with enough wrapping and adjustment. We've seen better systems for doubles that were tied around the cockpit rim with double fisherman's knots for adjusting. These better slings stayed on the cockpits at all times. Their knots allowed the slack to be taken up, and the small diameter of the line made it so low in profile that it didn't interfere with the sprayskirt rand.

Practice and experiment with different lengths and thicknesses of line to learn your personal preferences and enhance your use of the sling, whether in a self-rescue or an assisted rescue. Our criteria for slings, as well as all rescues that we turn to in real life, are simplicity and speed balanced with versatility.

Although it takes a few extra seconds to rig the sling, it's a great relief to have one if a person can't get onto his own deck or can't be dragged up onto his back deck by the shoulder of his PFD. Other options to try for swimmers having trouble climbing onto their kayaks are the My Deck/Your Deck technique and the Scoop Rescue, both described below.

■ Incapacitated Paddler Rescues: The Scoop and the Hand of God

If you ever need to rescue a paddler who is severely incapacitated, even a sling may be of little use. A swimmer who has dislocated a shoulder, for example, or who is so exhausted and/or hypothermic that he is floating in the water barely conscious (or even unconscious) won't be able to climb back into his cockpit no matter how many slings you rig. An even worse scenario might involve a paddler who has capsized but not yet wet exited. Anyone who is stuck upside down, too panicky and disoriented to release the sprayskirt, needs help fast. We hope you'll never face either of these situations in real life, but knowing the following two rescues—the Scoop and the Hand of God—could be a real lifesaver if you do.

Scoop Rescue

If she's cold and exhausted even a swimmer who isn't injured may not be able to get back into her cockpit no matter how much she struggles. We have occasionally seen this after multiple capsizes: A paddler who was able to reenter without trouble during an earlier capsize hits the water again and goes suddenly limp and confused. Sometimes it seems to take all her energy just to complete the first reentry (or second, or third), and she has nothing left for subsequent tries. At this point you may have no other option but to try a Scoop Rescue.

To Scoop someone basically involves tilting the empty kayak on its side and pushing it deep enough into the water that you can help the swimmer float her legs into the cockpit. After you get the floater shoved down into the cockpit as far as she'll go (floating on her side with her face out of the water), then right the kayak and start pumping. The name of this rescue comes from the idea that you will "scoop" the swimmer back into the kayak, but in reality what you scoop more than anything else is a whole lot of water.

Step by Step

Scoop Rescue

Step 1: Check In with the Swimmer

Talk with the person in the water. How is her state of mind? Make sure that she is not panicking before you approach. Make eye contact and talk to her before you get close enough for her to grab you. If the swimmer appears to be rattled and her eyes are wide and staring, you can be reassuring even beyond arms' reach. Try talking slowly, loudly, simply, and directly, using lots of repetition. For example, "Look at me. Look at me. I can help you. Calm down. Calm down." If you know her name, use it. Explain the procedure as you do it.

Step 2: Tilt the Empty Kayak

Bring your kayak parallel to the empty one and tilt it on its side, intentionally swamping her kayak so that it floats low in the water. This is one of the few rescues we find easier to do with the kayaks facing in the same direction.

Step 3: Scoop the Swimmer

Keep your paddle on your lap as you reach across the swimmer's kayak and start pushing her legs back into her cockpit. If her feet are not on her foot braces, that's fine; you want to slide her in so she's nice and low in the cockpit. At this point if the swimmer can give you even the slightest bit of help sliding into the cockpit, your job will be much easier.

Step 4: Right the Kayak

Once the swimmer's butt is more or less in her seat, push down on the side of her kayak that's nearest you. When the kayak starts to rotate, have the ex-swimmer lie back, then grab the shoulder of her PFD to lay her onto her back deck as you pull her up onto her kayak. Lowering her center of gravity in this way greatly facilitates righting the kayak.

Scoop Rescue: Step 3: Scoop the Swimmer—
Scoop the swimmer by working her legs into the cockpit.

Step 5: Drain the Kayak

Stabilize the kayak and start pumping out the water—the more pumps, the better. Assess your situation. Most likely this paddler will need more help to reach safety, such as some kind of stabilizing while being towed (see Chapter 8 for towing tips).

Given all the water that enters the cockpit along with the swimmer, this is a last-ditch rescue. If you can get her back in her boat any other way, do it. But if you can't, the Scoop is a good rescue to keep in the bottom of your bag of tricks in case all other methods have failed.

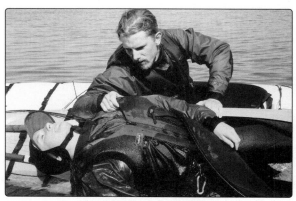

Step 4: Right the Kayak—
Right the kayak, laying the swimmer flat against the back deck to lower her center of gravity.

Hand of God Rescue

Occasionally someone capsizes without knowing how to wet exit or becomes disoriented and can't find the grab loop on the sprayskirt. We've heard of several paddlers who bailed out of their own kayaks to help someone who failed to wet exit. The problem with this solution is that it only adds another swimmer who needs to be rescued. Minimize the possibility of a novice getting stuck in the cockpit by giving her some instruction before she gets out on the water. But just in case your paddling partner forgets the wet exit lesson, here is a trick to save wet *non*exiters. It's called the Hand of God.

The name comes from the sensation of being delivered, if you are the lost soul who can't figure out how to wet exit, from the underwater darkness into the safety of daylight by a savior whom you can neither hear nor see. The person who is still right-side up needs to act quickly, by moving parallel to the overturned kayak. Once there, you pull the kayak to its side or all the way upright, depending on the size of the person trapped below.

Hand of God Rescue:
Step 2: Right the Kayak—
Right the kayak, pushing down on the near side as you pull up on the far side.

Step by Step

Hand of God

Step 1: Get the Boats Parallel

Pull alongside the capsized kayak. Move quickly but carefully: Be aware that if the swimmer remembers how to wet exit, her head could pop up. You don't want to meet hull to skull.

Step 2: Right the Kayak

Reach across the capsized kayak as far as possible with the hand that is nearest to it. Then use the same push-pull method that you employed to right the kayak in the Reenter and Pump Rescue: Push down with your near hand, pull up and toward you with the far hand.

Step 3: Resurrect the Paddler

As soon as the paddler's head appears, talk to the waterlogged mortal. Let her know that you are going to either right her kayak by laying her upper body onto her back deck (as in the Scoop Rescue) or release the sprayskirt for her so that she can slide out of her cockpit. In either case her head will stay up out of the water so that she can breathe.

The key in this important rescue is to act quickly. A normal wet exit takes less than three seconds. If you are watching someone who has failed to appear for more than ten seconds since her capsize, imagine what an eternity is passing below in the underwater darkness. Get moving— but don't leave the safety of your own kayak.

Step 3:
Resurrect the Paddler—
Resurrect the paddler,
pushing her flat
against the back deck
(or releasing her sprayskirt
if necessary).

My Deck/Your Deck

Not a full reentry by itself, this technique is an alternate way to help a swimmer who is experiencing difficulty climbing onto his back deck. Normally in this situation we'd first try other methods such as yanking on the swimmer's PFD to help him up onto his own deck, or using a Sling or a Scoop Rescue. If you don't have a sling and want to avoid all the water picked up in a Scoop Rescue, then you might try this.

The idea is to let the swimmer climb onto your stern deck first—the theory being that your deck will be lower in the water and easier for him to attain since it is being pushed down by the weight of you sitting in it. Once he is on your deck, he can then climb across to his own deck. This might come in particularly handy for rescuing double kayaks (or even some single designs) with very high decks. However, this technique requires that both kayaks face the *same direction.*

The problem with this is that your kayaks will normally be set up bow to stern facing in *opposite directions* (as recommended for any of the assisted reentries) when you discover that the swimmer can't get back into his kayak. Then you'll have to maneuver your own kayak around

180 degrees for this deck-to-deck transfer to work. If you have a second rescuer nearby, however, you could continue to stabilize in the facing position, while that person rafted up facing the same direction as the swimmer's boat for a My Deck/Your Deck assist.

■ Cleopatra's Needle and Other Flotation Problems

We have mentioned that adequate flotation is critical for safety. Every once in a while, a kayak with good flotation develops a problem, such as a blown hatch cover. (This is why some kayakers recommend using float bags, even if your kayak has bulkheads.) If you are alone when your kayak floods, get out your signaling devices: *You need help.* If you find someone else with flawed flotation, the Cleopatra's Needle Rescue and its variations provide some ways you might offer assistance.

This name *Cleopatra's Needle* comes from the mysterious way a fiberglass kayak can go completely vertical (poking like some giant needle into the sea) when one of its hatches floods. A plastic kayak may float less vertically, but the rescue steps are essentially the same. We'll start with a situation in which the front hatch is flooded.

Push down on the stern and pull up on the bow to begin draining the water.

Step by Step

Cleopatra's Needle Rescue

Step 1: Check In with the Swimmer

Talk with the swimmer and explain the procedure as you do it.

Step 2: Push the Stern Down

As strange as it sounds, if there is a bulkhead and the stern is still floating, push it down to force the flooded front hatch closer to the surface. Avoid pulling up on the stern to pry it onto the deck of your kayak, especially if either one of the kayaks is fiberglass. This kind of weight and leveraging could damage the boats, making a bad situation worse. With plastic kayaks you probably won't do any damage to the gear, just unnecessarily strain yourself.

Step 3: Continue to Push and Pull

As you push down on the stern, move your bow toward the sunken bow of the unfortunate kayak and alongside it. Ask the swimmer to travel hand over hand to your bow and reach into the

Cleopatra's Needle Rescue:
A flooded hatch causes the kayak to float vertically in the water like a needle poking into the sea.

REAL LIFE RESCUES

Jerry at the Lake

Jerry, an instructor friend of ours, teaches for a company that uses short recreational–style kayaks with large cockpits and no bulkheads on a small lake. He has worked out an interesting way to recover kayaks with little flotation. He teaches from a recreational double. When one of his students accidentally capsizes, he helps the swimmer get into the double with him, then they tow the swamped single kayak to shore. It's a lot of work for them both, but he has found it the easiest way to deal with a capsize when the kayak can't be reentered.

Roger + Jan

---

water to pull up as much as possible on the flooded end. To do this, he can either hold on to your bow with one hand for support, or lie over the top of it so he faces his own kayak. From across your deck, the swimmer can do a "curl" on the immersed kayak, bending his elbows into your deck and lifting the side of the swamped kayak's bow while you push down on the stern. Tilt the kayak on its side to get the water to start flowing out of the hatch and cockpit. The water will tend to move very slowly, but don't give up on this seemingly isometric exercise.

Other kayakers can help by rafting together to get the swimmer out of the water. With a group to help, one of the other kayakers does the curl across your bow as you push down on the floating end.

Step 4: Perform a T Rescue

Eventually you will be able to finish this rescue by draining the kayak with the T Rescue. If the hatch cover is still available, replacing it should fix the original problem. Otherwise you might try inflating a couple of paddlefloats in the open compartment and secure them with lines or bungees over the open hatch.

Variations on Cleopatra's Needle Rescue

Dealing with a Cleopatra's Needle is a little different if the rear hatch is flooded. In that case, push down on the bow to raise the flooded hatch. Unlike the situation of the front hatch flooding, the rear hatch will need to be resealed to get the cockpit drained. In a group, get the swimmer out of the water on a raft of decks and have him put weight on this floating end, so the rear hatch can be lifted and pumped.

What if there's no flotation? If the float bags or sea sock have failed for some reason, the stricken kayak may need to be towed to shore. In this case try either a Back Deck Swimmer Rescue, towing a raft with the extra boater on the back of two decks, or signal for help.

There are many ways to deal with flotation problems if there are people around. There are two main courses of action: either have a method to rectify the lack of flotation, or have enough power to tow the low-riding kayak to shore. There are very few options if you are alone.

■ Rescuing Loaded Sea Kayaks

When several days' food and camping gear are crammed into your hatches, doing a rescue can become a bit more complicated. The extra weight of a loaded boat makes it more difficult to manipulate, and the combination of the load along with a swamped cockpit can seriously reduce the kayak's *freeboard*—the nautical term for the vertical distance between the waterline and the deck. There are times when a loaded kayak plus paddler plus water in the cockpit sinks your kayak so low that the sea can wash in over the coaming faster than you can pump it out. (For information on rescuing loaded doubles, see page 97.)

Self-Rescues for Loaded Sea Kayaks

Even with a fully loaded boat, a nice, slow, clean Eskimo Roll is possible. The secret to a successful roll with a heavy craft is in your knees. Good technique is essential: If your lower body initiates some momentum for the mass of ballast around it, your head and torso can barely help but follow. Avoid trying to muscle your way up with just your paddle.

If you have to wet exit, the Scramble should be a little easier than usual, because the weight gives your kayak lowness and increased stability. The Paddlefloat Rescue would be one of your best options, and it can give you a stable platform to work from while you pump like crazy. The Reenter and Roll will get you right-side up, but there will be more water in the cockpit than with any of the rescues listed above—not a good thing with a loaded kayak.

Assisted Reentry Techniques for Loaded Sea Kayaks

If the kayak has bulkheads fore and aft and if the swimmer is able to assist with the T Rescue, there's no problem: Just do the T Rescue and get

the swimmer back into the loaded kayak. Some people believe that with all that weight in the bow, it will be impossible to lift it up for a T Rescue. Remember that at least half the weight of the loaded boat should be in the stern; preferably, closer to two–thirds of the overall weight should be behind the cockpit. Think back to your childhood days on the seesaw, and imagine your big sister on the other seat. Did she have any trouble popping you up into the air? If your swimmer shoves his weight down onto the stern of that overturned bulkheaded kayak, its bow can pop right up in your face.

If the water is choppy and you are working on an overturned kayak without bulkheads, you'd better hope that your swimmer has a tight sprayskirt to put on his coaming when you do the Reenter and Pump. If he does, you can replace the sprayskirt and put the pump down one side or even sometimes down the body tube to pump out.

Rafting up to stabilize the swamped boat and towing it, with passenger, to shore is another option. In-line towing (see Chapter 8 for a description) with multiple muscular motors attached to the swamped kayak would be the easiest way to go. The members of the tow team can rotate their field positions with towing and stabilizing if they become tired.

■ Double Reentries

Although double kayaks may appear to be safer because they are more stable (especially loaded with camping gear) and less likely to tip over in the first place, they can still capsize. When they do, you will generally have a much higher volume of water and greater weight and size overall to deal with. However, most of the reentries and recoveries for doubles are basically modified versions of the same ones that work for singles. We'll start with some tips for the times when you and your paddling partner need to reenter on your own and then share some ideas for giving assistance to a capsized double that you aren't in.

Righting a Double Kayak from the Water

After you and your partner wet exit, quickly communicate your plan for recovery of your craft. If you have one or two paddlefloats, you will want to leave the kayak upside down while you put the paddlefloat on, secure it, and inflate it. If you are going to try a double Scramble, the kayak needs to be righted.

One way to flip a double is similar to the righting of a single. Both swimmers will need to be on the same side of the kayak, at their cockpits. Each swimmer reaches under the kayak to firmly grasp the coaming on both sides. Simultaneously, they push the near side of the coaming up and away while pulling the far side of the coaming toward themselves.

An option called the Capistrano Flip was developed by canoeists for righting overturned canoes, but it works with some double sea kayaks. Two swimmers need to get under the kayak with their heads in the cockpits, grasping the coaming on each side of the kayak. Together they vigorously use an egg-beater-style kick or frog kick to raise up the kayak and twist it over their heads to the same side. Because the cockpits occasionally create suction that resists lifting straight up, try tilting the kayak as you lift. In a totally different approach, paddlers start on the same side of the overturned kayak and try to get across and on top of it. Then they grasp the side away from themselves and pull it into the righted position as they lean back and away from the side they are holding. But this final method scoops the greatest amount of water, because the weight of the two paddlers on the hull pushes the cockpit deeper into the water as it rolls over. So we don't recommend it as a first option.

Double Self-Rescue Choices

So much depends on the style of kayak, the size and strength of each paddler, and the conditions. Without a doubt, having at least one paddlefloat along will give you more recovery options; having two along can maximize your stability.

Simultaneous Paddlefloat Reentry

The paddlefloat devices can be attached and inflated while the swimmers are on the same side, feet in each cockpit, kayak upside down. The kayak needs to be righted, as described above, while the swimmers are on the same side of it. Then one swimmer will need to move around to the opposite side. Setting up your paddlefloats on each side of the kayak will create counterbalancing outriggers. Approaching from opposite sides, each paddler follows through with her own Paddlefloat Self-Rescue as described for the single kayak in Chapter 5. Some paddlers prefer to do simultaneous Paddlefloat Rescues from the same side; although they might lose some stability, the deck is lower and easier to climb onto because both their weight is on one side.

Simultaneous Paddlefloat Reentry:
Swimmers reenter from opposite sides of a double kayak while their paddlefloats provide balance.

REAL LIFE RESCUES

Reentry at Punta Diablo

The six of us eat breakfast quickly and pack our boats in the dark, a common practice on long kayaking trips in Baja, where you want to avoid paddling in the afternoon winds. We are all a little nervous, knowing that we have to round a major exposed point, some 5 miles ahead in the dark, before we make it into the protection of Bahía de San Juanico. The point is a ½ mile of sheer cliff rising some 200 feet out of the water, preceded by a mile of steep, cobble beach. The cliff collects the incoming wind waves and bounces them right back out at the Sea of Cortez without absorbing any of the energy. The locals call it Punta Diablo—Devil's Point. We'll give it a wide berth.

The seas have already been stirred up into 4 to 6 feet of steep, confused chop by several days of intermittent, 20- to 25-knot winds. By midmorning we're still a mile from Punta Diablo, and the whitecaps all around tell us today's freshening breeze has already picked up to 15 knots. We keep our little group close together and moving as quickly as possible. As we near the point, the seas become even more confused from the waves rebounding off the cliffs.

Ted moves out in the lead. He's a strong paddler with well-practiced reentry skills, but today he's struggling with the flu. Suddenly he's over and slapping his hull for an Eskimo Bow Rescue. Jan pushes her loaded kayak as quickly as possible, but trying to sprint with such a load is too slow. She arrives well after Ted wet exits. "Hang on to your boat," she calls out. If he lets go of his kayak in these conditions, she knows, we could have trouble finishing the rescue before Ted and his boat wash into the rocky cliffs.

Ted's response sounds tired, even overrehearsed: "I am." Keeping an eye on the cliffs, Jan reaches for his bow, and Ted pushes his upper body up onto the stern, straight-arming the kayak with both hands, his paddle pinned in his underarm. Ted's bow pops up in the air, and Jan pulls it across her deck until she can reach his coaming. Together they spin it, but they see that the cockpit scoops water. They quickly set up to try again. This second time Ted gets off the kayak before it spins, and Jan is able to time the flip to avoid the peaks of the confused seas. She leans over to stabilize his boat, and within seconds he is back in the cockpit, replacing his sprayskirt.

Ted's kayak still has a little water in it, but rather than take the time to pump, or risk another capsize, we raft him up with his wife to stabilize him. Roger hooks his tow line onto Ted's bow and starts towing them both quickly toward the calmer water that we know lies just beyond Punta Diablo. Within a few hundred yards of the capsize, the water begins to flatten out and we all start to relax. In the lee of the point, behind the Devil's back, we get the chance we need to catch our breaths and collect our thoughts before pushing on to the next serene beach we'll call home for another day.

Roger + Jan

Sequential (One-at-a-Time) Paddlefloat Reentry

There are a couple of different sequences that can be employed here. In one method, one swimmer helps to stabilize the kayak while the other performs the Paddlefloat Self-Rescue. Then the second swimmer can borrow the paddlefloat device, or use one of her own, or just climb in while the seated person stabilizes with the paddlefloat. In another option, one paddler stays in the water to stabilize the kayak for the other. After the first paddler is back in her seat, the swimmer sets up a Paddlefloat Rescue. In lieu of or in addition to the paddlefloat, the paddler in the kayak helps counterbalance by doing a Sculling Brace. If you both have paddlefloats, you can still run a sequence: The first one in keeps leaning on her paddlefloat to continue stabilizing for her partner. By performing the technique in sequence, the swimmers can stay on the same side and encourage each other throughout the reentry. Different sequences will work best for different paddling partners and the particular kayak that you are in.

Double Scrambles: Simultaneous and Sequential

One version of the Scramble is for both swimmers to reenter their cockpits simultaneously but on opposite sides. Placement and

Sequential Double Scramble: Step 1:
One person climbs into the cockpit, while the other stabilizes the kayak from the water.

Simultaneous Double Scramble:
Paddlers climb up on opposite sides at the same time to counterbalance the kayak.

Step 2:
Once the first swimmer has reentered, she can use a sculling brace to stabilize the kayak for the second swimmer's reentry.

timing of the crux move together are crucial: You must make the move of swimming up and pulling across the deck in the same moment and opposing each other to help counterbalance the kayak. For doubles, the Taco Scramble—where you get up across the cockpit and then spin and drop your derriere right into the seat—might work better than the Cowboy Scramble, in which you straddle the kayak like a rider mounting a horse. Most doubles are so wide that people sitting astride one can't get their legs down into the water to act as stabilizers. Also, the double cockpits are sized to give you more room to maneuver your legs when you have your bum in the seat.

You can also try Scrambles in sequence, with one person climbing into the cockpit while the other helps stabilize the kayak from the water. Once the first swimmer has reentered, she can use a Sculling Brace to stabilize the kayak while the second climbs into his cockpit. We have found that this sometimes works best if the person in the rear cockpit reenters first. If you are in the water, it may be easier to stabilize a kayak from the bow. Some people recommend that the person who is generally having the more difficult time get in first, and then the other person can hop up.

Other Options

Eskimo Rolling is also possible in a double. Both paddlers need to set up on the same side, and ideally the bow person initiates the roll, but if the timing is pretty close and the technique is clean, the double will roll. Reenter and Roll can also work for partners who share strong skills and teamwork. As for all of the reentries, practice will help you discover the best methods for you. For reentries with doubles, repetition will hone the requisite teamwork of you and your paddling partner.

Assisted Reentry Techniques for Doubles

T Rescues are manageable for doubles with rear bulkheads; they're easier if there are also compartments in the bow and between the cockpits. If you are T Rescuing a double, make sure that both swimmers keep in contact with their kayak while you manipulate it. Ask them both to push down on the stern to help you raise the bow. If there is at least one other rescue boat, the Assisted T Rescue is even better for rescuing doubles with rear bulkheads. The extra assistant can

The T Rescue can be done on a double kayak. Note both swimmers pushing down on the stern to help raise the bow.

help lift the kayak bow extra high to accommodate the overall length as well as the proximity of the rear cockpit relative to the stern.

If either swimmer cannot tolerate being in the water, forget the water-draining exercise and just get them back into their kayak, one at a time, with the Reenter and Pump. Even a Scoop Reentry may be employed if a swimmer is having trouble making the cockpit with a sling or any of the other methods. Once the swimmers are in, everyone who can reach in should start pumping. There will be lots of water, so the more pumps, the merrier.

Helping Right a Double from Another Kayak

To help right the kayak from your kayak, as in preparing for a Reenter and Pump, ask the two swimmers to get to the same side of the kayak, then paddle up to the side that they are not on. When you are opposite the swimmers, lean over their kayak and grasp the far side and the near side of the overturned hull. Push down on the near side and pull up on the far side, just as you would for a single kayak. If the swimmers can help you, encourage them to push and pull on the cockpit coaming at the same time. From the water they need to push up and over on the side nearest themselves while they pull on the side nearest you. They will be reaching under the kayak while you are working on the hull, which is facing the sky. If they can't help you, they need to continue to hold on to their paddles and kayak.

If someone capsizes and has not yet wet exited, you should try the Hand of God Rescue, or else reach underwater to the overturned cockpits, release the sprayskirts, and pull the people out. In either case, to release people from their cockpits, do not leave your own (unless, of course, you are in the double with one of them).

Hints for Getting a Swimmer Up and Across the Double Kayak

Getting up onto a double from the water is a big challenge. Compared to a single, the deck of a double tends to float much higher—unless it is *seriously* swamped with water, as sometimes happens without bulkheads or with minimal air space. Jan has practiced getting up onto the upper deck, across from a tired partner, pulling on the shoulders of his PFD as she slid back into the water away from him. As she hung on to him and he kicked hard, he slid up onto the deck as she slid off.

Here's an interesting idea we once used with a group of differently abled paddlers. The swimmer with control of her legs used the paddlefloat and sling as part of her support and leverage while she more or less stood on the paddle shaft and sling that had the paddlefloat attached. From this outrigger, she helped push a paraplegic swimmer onto the deck and the swimmer's awkward legs back down into the cockpit. Because of the additional height of the upper decks on doubles, slings have great application for many paddlers. We've seen stirrups set up somewhat permanently on either back decks or around cockpits. For the extra height of the deck on doubles, it's great to be able to use your legs for a boost up and out of the water.

Rescue Tips for Loaded Double Sea Kayaks

When we have to rescue a double kayak full of camping gear, we hope that it has bulkheads at least in the mid- and aft sections, and preferably in the bow as well. If there are no other kayaks around and rescue is up to just you and your paddling partner, work together to right it with the push-pull system or climb up on the overturned hull together and pull it toward you simultaneously. Go ahead and do a Scramble to get in; it will be pretty low in the water. Some of the popular touring doubles hold so much water that they can ride very low even without the additional weight of expedition gear. If you are caught without any paddling buddies to help you and you are taking on water faster than you can pump, signal for outside assistance. If you have enough people around for an assisted rescue, do your best with a

Reenter and Pump, then stabilize the swamped craft and tow it to shore while pumping with as many friends as possible.

■ Sit-on-Top Kayaks

Sit-on-top, or open-deck, kayaks have no cockpit to sit inside. Sitting up on *top* of these kayaks rather than down *inside* of them raises your center of gravity. To compensate, sit-on-tops are generally much wider and boxier than cockpit boats. Some people consider these kayaks safer than cockpit kayaks, because they don't have to learn "special rescue skills." However, you must still heed the same precautions about the water and weather to stay safe. We offer some tips to make the experience of a capsize recovery go a little more smoothly for folks who paddle sit-on-tops, or for the times when these boats are part of your group and you want to give someone a hand.

Self-Recovery for a Sit-on-Top

To get back into the paddling position, you will first need to flip the kayak right-side up, using the push-pull method previously described for righting kayaks. Don't push up just one side; it may simply drop back down on your head. You can also climb up on the overturned hull, grab the edge on the side away from you, and then slide back into the water, pulling the edge over with you. For double sit-on-tops, either method will work, but both swimmers need to be on the same side.

Keeping the kayak flat while you get back on it is the big challenge. Grasp the two sides of the kayak just in front of the seat. The hand that is farther from you needs to hold that side down. For a double sit-on-top, swimmers can start on opposite sides.

Kick your legs to the surface and out behind you. Time a good strong kick with pushing the flat kayak down and under you. Pushing the kayak under you with your hands isn't cheating, just putting the odds in your favor—it's not

easy climbing onto things floating in the water.

Once you are balanced just forward of the seat on your belly, wait a moment to catch your breath. Slowly roll over on your backside, plant your hips into the seat, and swing your legs back into their forward position.

Assisted Reentry for Sit-on-Tops

You can make the life of a sit-on-top's swimmer much easier if you can hold his kayak flat for him while he climbs aboard. If the kayak is not yet righted, then you reach over the hull while you are alongside and opposite the swimmer. Time your push-pulls together to flip the kayak over. Stabilize by leaning across the two paddles that are in a bridge across your kayak as you would for a regular kayak. The kayaks can face bow to stern or bow to bow. There is no cockpit to hold on to, but the upper edges of the deck make firm points of contact.

The swimmer will launch up and out of the water in front of the seat of the sit-on-top and then roll into it. If he has any trouble with this move, reach across and pull on his PFD. Continue to stabilize until he is back into the paddling position. If you're assisting a double, have the swimmers stay on same side and get back in their seats one at a time.

Any kayaking assistant can be very helpful for holding a kayak flat, and can sometimes even help pull someone back onto his boat. Just a couple of more good reasons to paddle with a buddy, no matter how "safe" we think our kayaks are.

■ Rescues in Surf, Rock Gardens, and Rough Water

You need to be ready to perform rescues in whatever conditions you kayak in. So if you enjoy the excitement of open-coast paddling, you'll want to prepare yourself to meet the demands of dealing with capsizes in challenging seas. The following techniques are ones we use

Caves are enticing to explore but they create rough water conditions that make rescues more risky.

in surf, rock gardens, sea caves, and other dynamic, rough-water situations.

Surf Rescues

The usual advice for assisted rescues in the surf is "don't." You are likely to just make a bad situation worse. By charging in to help out a capsized paddler in the surf zone, you not only risk becoming a swimmer yourself but also risk injuring the swimmer and damaging gear by bringing an additional kayak into the waves nearby.

With these warnings firmly in mind, however, some expert paddlers *with bombproof combat rolls and excellent boat control in the surf* may want to consider the circumstances when the risk of assisting a swimmer in the surf may be justified. There are also some actions that surf-zone swimmers can take to help themselves.

If you capsize in the surf, you can generally swim and wade your boat ashore, being careful to stay to seaward of the kayak. One way to facilitate this in deep water is to put your kayak parallel to shore and hang on to the cockpit, allowing the waves to wash you into the shallows. If you capsize on the outer edge of a wide surf zone and are facing a long swim to shore, however, the better choice may be to swim your boat out beyond the break zone and do a deep-water reentry. To "swim-tow" your boat, grab the bow toggle and your paddle in one hand to free your other hand for swimming. Keep a loose grip on your kayak when attempting this; if a big wave tries to rip your boat from your grasp, let it go. We have seen fingers broken and arms injured from swimmers holding their boats too tightly in the surf. Don't expect to be able to move very fast this way, and do expect to become exhausted quickly. If there are lulls between waves, you might have time to reenter your kayak, assuming you are able to do a quick Scramble Rescue or a Reenter and Roll. It is unlikely that you'll have time to rig a paddlefloat in most surf zones, however.

If you are in your kayak watching a paddling partner take a long swim, you might be able to help, assuming you have the requisite skills and are feeling very, very lucky. We have tried paddling in quickly to offer a stern toggle to the swimmer who is swim-towing her kayak. As discussed in the following chapter, towing a swimmer is not very efficient. Don't expect to move very fast, and make sure that the swimmer understands that she must let go immediately if a wave comes and you need to get out of Dodge. If you are able to tow the swimmer out to safer waters to do a T Rescue, just make sure you have time to finish the reentry before you drift back into the surf zone. Under no circumstances do we recommend rigging a tow rope in any kind of surf because of the possibility of becoming tangled in the line.

We also can't recommend trying assisted rescues, though Roger has had some success doing both quick T Rescues and Bow Rescues in the middle of a surf zone. (He has also had some fantastic wipeouts and has broken a paddle while learning when *not* to try this.) On the occasions when it worked, he was very fast, kept his bow pointed into the waves, and was able to abandon the rescue attempt quickly in order to paddle out through approaching waves without getting washed back into the swimmer. It sometimes took several attempts to finish the rescue. One thing he can definitely recommend not doing: If a wave is coming, don't try to raft up sideways with the swimmer once she's back in her cockpit and expect to be able to side-surf together toward shore. The kayaks will likely just tumble over each other, and you'll be lucky not to get hurt.

Rock Garden Rescues

If the surf is breaking through a rock garden or into a sea cave, the dangers increase exponentially. So should your caution. Basically the same techniques apply as used in the surf zone: swim-towing, toggle towing, and quick self- or assisted rescues. Dangerous as they can be, rocks can also create refuges in their lee where you can bring a kayak to do a rescue. But instead of thinking about what kind of dicey rescues you might be able to pull off in big surf and rock gardens, we'd

Sometimes it is necessary to "toggle-tow" a swimmer and kayak to a safer location before beginning a reentry.

recommend avoiding those areas until you develop a bombproof Eskimo Roll.

Rough Water

We've found that successful rescues in rough water require good technique and good concentration. One of the keys is to make sure to hang on to your kayak and paddle. If you let go for even a second, they could quickly wash out of reach. We also suggest that you keep your paddlefloat and pump secure but handy, and stow or tether loose gear in your cockpit so it won't become flotsam in a capsize. If you wet exit in rough water, you'll have your hands full enough without having to worry about a bunch of floating

"yard sale items" such as water bottles, dry bags, sunscreen, and paddlefloats.

Maneuvering in rough seas can be difficult. Try to use the choppy water to your advantage instead of fighting it. If you are trying to T Rescue a bow that is bouncing up and down on the waves, for example, grab it on the upswing, letting the water do the work of lifting it for you. But watch out that you don't get hit in the face with a bouncing bow. Be deliberate and careful so the rescue gets done right on the first attempt. Do your best to relax and stay focused on what needs to get done. If you tense up or rush, you'll only get sloppy and make things harder on yourself.

■ Chapter 8
Keeping It All Together

■ Towing Skills
■ Retrieval of Boats and Swimmers

So what can you do if someone gets tired, gets injured, or loses his kayak after a capsize? This chapter mixes the nuts and bolts of towing—psychology, strategy, technique, and gear—with tips for dealing with swimmers who've let go of their boats. Whether you're trying to keep a group of paddlers together on the water or you need to reunite a swimmer with his boat, the techniques in this chapter can help you avert mayhem and turn a potential "mayday" into a "Thanks, man," (or "Thanks, ma'am" as the case may be).

■ Towing Skills

Towing may not be a rescue in the "capsize recovery" sense, but since it can involve extricating someone from a difficult or even dangerous situation, it can be a rescue in the *true* sense of the word. Ideally, though, you can use towing well ahead of time to prevent a paddler from getting exhausted and having to be fished out of the water in the first place. Towing can also be used in conjunction with a reentry to pull those involved away from a dangerous area while the reentry is still in progress. (See Real Life Rescue—Southerly Blow at Point Lobos.) Given the number of reasons you might need them, having both a tow line and the ability to use it quickly and efficiently is an extemely valuable safety tool. Towing is easy to learn, and we strongly recommend that paddlers at every level add this essential skill to their rescue "tool kits."

On the surface, towing may seem little more than a simple feat of brute strength: Just hook up and go. But there is more to towing than simply lashing on a length of line and slogging into the wind. Many subtleties are involved, subtleties that can make the difference between a successful run-of-the-mill tow job and a tangled mess of line. When the wind is howling offshore, your partner is seasick or exhausted, and the seas are raging, it's not the time to pull out your tow line for the first time and try to figure out where to attach the ends, how quickly you can hook up, or how much energy will be required. By familiarizing yourself with your towing system beforehand and practicing the following solo and tandem towing techniques in a variety of conditions, you'll be able to tow more effectively when you really need to.

For example, let's say it's Saturday morning and you and your paddling buddy are headed back to the car for lunch; or maybe you're island-hopping in Baja on a glorious day, sunny and hot, but a breeze wafting down out of the sierra keeps you nice and cool. With only a mile or two separating you from camp, your partner starts lagging behind. You notice that he is tired, so you rest for a while, but then you realize that the nice cooling breeze is beginning to blow you backward. You offer your water bottle along with some words of encouragement, and soon you are on the move again, but slowly. At this pace, you realize, it could take hours to reach camp, and your hungry stomach rumbles its complaint. If you only had a tow rope, it could speed you both to a real meal, but for the time being you munch a granola bar and keep slogging.

Now let's say your partner is not only tired but has tendinitis (or seasickness, or blisters) and begins wincing in pain with every stroke. Maybe the cooling breeze starts gusting to 20 knots offshore and your buddy is being blown backward across the Sea of Cortez—next stop Mazatlán, 100 miles over the horizon. Bummer. Suddenly the lack of a tow rope is no mere inconvenience.

Sure, we're being melodramatic, but having a tow rope is at least a convenience, and in an emergency it could save lives. Yet this essential piece of safety gear is often overlooked. That's too bad, because unlike all the other safety stuff we cart around diligently and (knock on wood) rarely if ever use—flares, spare paddles, first-aid kit—we use our tow ropes all the time. Typically we use them to pull our way out of pickles no more threatening than needing to speed up a tired paddler who's putting off lunch. But towing has also saved our aft ends on occasion by keeping us out of more serious predicaments—such as accelerating an open-water crossing so that we reached land before dark, or before a storm hit, or before the tide turned against us. We've also attached tow lines to kayaks in the midst of T Rescues on the open ocean to prevent anyone from being swept into the cliffs before the rescue was finished. In times like those a simple tow line may well have made the difference between our getting to shore safely and being caught in the pages of a *Sea Kayaker* magazine incident report.

When to Tow and the Psychology of Towing

There are endless reasons to tow. If someone is totally exhausted or injured, it's obviously time to drag out your tow rope. But other situations may not be so cut and dried—for example, if you're trying to keep a group from getting too spread out across the water, even if it's a group of only two paddlers. A tired paddler slowing down a group so that it's a few minutes late for lunch is one thing. But missing lunch entirely is quite another; so is getting caught out after dark or in the path of an approaching storm. In such situations the adage "A group travels only as fast as its slowest paddlers" does not preclude doing something to speed up the slow ones. If a paddler—or paddlers—can't pick up the pace when necessary, it's better to start towing *before* they become totally exhausted.

For smooth, efficient towing, technique and finesse are required to handle not only the tow line but also the feelings of the towed paddler. Since human nature seems to resist wanting to admit that you're having trouble keeping up with your partners, a certain psychology of towing is often involved.

Sometimes the hardest part about towing is convincing a lagging paddler that towing is in everyone's best interest. Whether from pride or not wanting to be a burden, people often decline offers to be towed. We once watched a paddler adamantly refuse towing assistance even as a strong side wind was blowing her onto a vast mudflat at dusk on a falling tide. By slowing our pace to let her catch up, the rest of us in the group were getting blown toward the same mudflat. Our only options were to leave her behind to spend the night alone in the mud, to spend the night in the mud with her, or to tow. Unfortunately, there was little time at that moment for explanations, so her loud cursing had to be ignored as we clipped a tow line to her bow and pulled her to the safety of deeper water.

A situation like this is less a matter of *asking* a paddler if she'd like a tow than of *telling* her it's time to be towed. A little face-saving diplomacy, however, can go a long way. When approaching a potentially resistant paddler, for example, you may be tempted to say, "Look, damnit, it's getting dark, I'm cold and hungry, and I'd much rather tow you than wait for you." Don't do it. We've learned instead to simply explain the need for speed, and we try not to make towing seem like the end of the line, as if we were hooking up a broken-down car to be hauled off to the dump. We've had better luck melting resistance by avoiding the T-word entirely. "We're going to give you a *boost*," we say, "just a *short rest* until we catch up to the group" (or cross a swift current, or reach the lee of an island). We encourage her to help out by paddling as much as possible, and let her know that we'll unhitch as soon as possible.

Also, the best time to raise the towing specter is well beforehand, on shore. After the mudflat incident, we have found that if we explain to a group ahead of time that under certain conditions we might need to tow to keep everyone safe and comfortable, we tend to get better cooperation later if we have to pull out our tow ropes.

Towing can often be avoided in the planning stages of a trip, by choosing a route well within the abilities of each individual. But if more experienced paddlers knowingly drag beginners along on longer trips, they may end up having to drag those neophytes, literally, at the end of a tow line. This can be fine if the plan is communicated clearly so everyone understands beforehand what they are getting themselves into. We once spent a week in the San Juan Islands with two friends—one a triathlete looking for a challenging workout, her friend a couch potato who liked good scenery if she didn't have to work too hard to get it. We were all in single kayaks, so we used a tow line to create a tandem kayak. The triathlete got a great workout towing her friend through a series of 15-mile days; the friend got to see a lot of scenery without having to work too hard. Both were happy. But if this sort of compromise is not worked out ahead of time, it can end up being a real drag for the paddlers at both ends of the tow line.

In groups we often prefer to get several paddlers involved with an In-Line Towing exercise (three or more paddlers in a row, linked by tow ropes like a train). Not only is this easier for those towing (more engines), but it also helps minimize the chance of anyone feeling singled out. When leading our annual expeditions in Baja and the San Juan Islands, we sometimes use In-Line Towing during long, open-water crossings between islands. This keeps the group together and moving as quickly as possible, shortening the overall time of the crossing and minimizing our exposure. By practicing this on flat water beforehand, our students learn a valuable skill and we work out any bugs in the system as a group, so that we can set up a tow line quickly and efficiently when we really need it.

When *Not* to Tow

One downside to towing is that the paddler doing the towing will be somewhat tied up. In rough water, for example, you may not want the strongest paddler in your group hooked up to a tow line if that person is also the best one to deal with rescuing a capsized paddler. You should also avoid towing in the surf zone. It's extremely hazardous to be tied to another kayak in breaking waves.

Step by Step
Basic Towing Technique

There are many ways to tow: Single Tows, various types of team tows, even a Contact Tow that uses no tow line at all. And there are as many types of towing systems, from a simple hank of rope to waist belts to integrated rescue vests replete with carabiners, quick-release harnesses, and shock-absorbing bungees. No matter which of the following techniques (with the exception of the ropeless Contact Tow) or which gear you use, the basic components of towing are the same—hooking up, paying out line, and unhooking and stowing your line. Fairly simple to rig if you pay attention to details, tow lines are also fairly easy to tangle up if you don't. Here are a few tips to help you set up a tow quickly and efficiently and avoid ending up with a lap full of spaghetti.

Step 1: Hooking Up

Regardless of which towing technique you are using, paddle up to the bow of the boat you are going to tow so that you can lean on it for support while you attach the line to the bow toggle. Stabilizing yourself this way is especially useful in rough water. A carabiner is probably the quickest and easiest form of attachment. If you are good at knots, however, you might tie a bowline. We have also used a simple loop (made with a figure-8 knot) to quickly girth hitch a T-shaped bow toggle (but it won't work if the bow handle is a loop). To girth hitch a toggle, run the tow-line loop through the bow loop, then wrap each side of the tow-line loop up and over each side of the T-toggle.

The other end of the tow line should already be attached to the person towing or the middle of his kayak with some type of quick-release system, so it can be unhitched quickly in an emergency. See Gear for Towing, below, for more information on types of towing systems, including waist belts and boat-based styles.

Here's a tip: Don't tie a line to your stern toggle. There are two reasons for this. First, you won't be able to reach it to undo it in an emergency; also, towing from the stern is much less efficient than towing from the center of your kayak. A line that's attached to the back of your boat tends to jerk your stern from side to side every time it gets pulled taut, making steering difficult.

Step 2: Paying Out Line

After hooking up, paddle away carefully at first, paying attention to where the line is and how it is paying out. Generally the line will take care of itself, but we have seen people start paddling in too big a hurry and get loose line wrapped all around their paddles or tangled in their back-deck rigging and rudders. If you start paddling away slowly at first, you can avoid not only tangling the line, but also the sudden jerk when the line goes taut.

Once the line is paid out and taut, try to keep some tension on it, even if you stop to rest, to avoid getting tangled in the loose line. Up or down, rudders are especially good at getting fouled in tow lines. Although we generally prefer to paddle with-

Basic Towing Technique:
Step 1: Hooking Up—
Lean on the bow for support, while connecting the tow line.

Step 3: Unhooking and Stowing a Tow Line—
Flake the line to avoid tangles.

out using our rudders, we have found that they make steering and tracking easier when towing.

Step 3: Unhooking and Stowing a Tow Line

When you are ready to unhook the line, you may need to do so quickly. If a strong wind is blowing or a current is running, you don't want to drift backward while unhooking and lose all the hard-won ground (water?) you just gained.

Here's a useful tip: The tow line will be running on one side of your stern or the other, and we've found it easier to turn to that side before pulling in line. Have the paddler aim his bow at your cockpit so you can lean on it again while you undo the tow line. As soon as you're unhooked, you may want to urge the paddler to continue, so he doesn't lose ground.

Depending on the type of tow system being used, we generally have better luck avoiding tangles if we *flake* the line instead of wrapping it around our hand before stuffing it in its stow bag. Flaking involves gathering the line in a series of S-shaped bends instead of wrapping it in circular loops. Flaked line tends to pay out more cleanly the next time it's used, while loops tend to tangle.

If you are in a hurry to continue paddling, it is tempting to just pile the line in your lap and deal with it later. Be very careful if you do this. You are inviting a tangled mess, especially if you happen to capsize with 30 feet of loose line in your lap. We prefer tow systems that can be stowed quickly on the water (see Gear for Towing, below).

Jan occasionally stows her tow line down the front of her PFD or under her front-deck bungees. While this keeps the loose line somewhat out of the way, it could still cause problems in a capsize.

Techniques for One-Paddler Towing

One-Paddler Towing is not about towing yourself, it is about one paddler towing another. We'll start with the simplest techniques, and get to the gear later, after group towing is discussed. (In the meantime, consider the old philosophical question about the sound of one paddler towing—if no one is around to hear him, does he make a sound?)

Contact Tow: Towing Without a Rope

Not really a tow per se, but more of a push, a Contact Tow can be useful if you don't have far to tow or don't have a tow line. Essentially the

Contact Tow:
This tow uses no rope and at times is more like a forward push.

person needing the tow simply grabs on to your bow or stern, forming a two-person raft, while you push or pull him with your boat. We have used this to tow paddlers away from a rock, pier, or other hazard, and to retrieve a dropped paddle. A Contact Tow can also be used to support an incapacitated paddler during towing, but hopefully you won't have far to go, because both steering control and forward progress are awkward with someone hanging on to your kayak.

There are three main configurations for contact tows, and which method works best depends on the kayaks being used. First, the paddler being towed can hang on to your bow facing forward (so that essentially you are *pushing* him rather than towing). This works best if you have a long bow and his boat has a short, narrow stern. Otherwise his stern may get in the way of your stroke on one side. Second, you can have the towee face backward off your bow. This might give you more room to paddle if his bow is skinnier than his stern. The last way is to have him face forward while hanging on to your stern—a good method if he has a short, narrow bow. Whichever method you try, the person being towed must keep the kayaks parallel and as close together as possible. If the kayaks start drifting apart at an angle, progress will become increasingly difficult.

Single Tow

Once you've convinced someone to accept a tow, the simplest configuration to use is the Single Tow. Simply attach your line to his bow, pay it out carefully, and begin paddling. The main trick here is to pace yourself so you don't end up becoming exhausted and needing a tow yourself. Remind the towed paddler that his job is to keep his boat in as straight a line as possible behind you and to help out by paddling as much as he can without becoming exhausted. If either kayak has a rudder, now is a good time to use it to help keep the boats in line—but try to keep the line taut to avoid tangling it in the rudders.

The Single Tow is the best option for a lone pair of paddlers, since it is essentially their only option. Its only advantage for groups of three or more is that it is quick to set up and won't complicate matters be requiring teamwork. However, since towing by yourself can be tiring and slow, Single Towing is not always the most efficient use of group resources. So it is a good idea to practice team towing techniques as well.

Single Tow:
This is the simplest towing configuration.

Team Towing Techniques for Two or More Paddlers

"Two heads are better than one," captures the essence of the synergy people gain when bouncing ideas off of one another. We've seen its counterpart with towing into the wind. When people have someone to share the workload with there is less strain for each and they tend to encourage each other through difficult stretches.

In-Line Towing

This is our preferred method for including more engines during towing. Basically it involves linking several paddlers in a line. We find it simpler to perform than the side-by-side arrangements listed below, especially for less experienced paddlers.

Because the lead position takes the most effort (think of a pack of bike racers drafting off one another), put the strongest paddler in front, then the second strongest, then the third, and so on, in descending order. Over longer distances the lead positions can be alternated to share the load.

We generally don't put more than four paddlers in a line, because communication becomes difficult. With larger groups, we usually try to split into teams of equal strength. We also like to leave at least one paddler out of the tow line(s) when possible to de-liver messages from one end of the line to the other or to help if a tow rope gets tangled in a rudder.

V-Tow

Splitting the load between two paddlers in a V-configuration is less work for each, but it requires good teamwork and boat-handling skills. If one paddler is stronger than the other, she'll do all the towing while the weaker paddler's tow line stays slack. Another challenge during a V-Tow is for the paddlers to stay far enough apart that they don't bump into each other, but not so far apart that the V spreads into a flat line. This method is made easier if both tow boats have rudders.

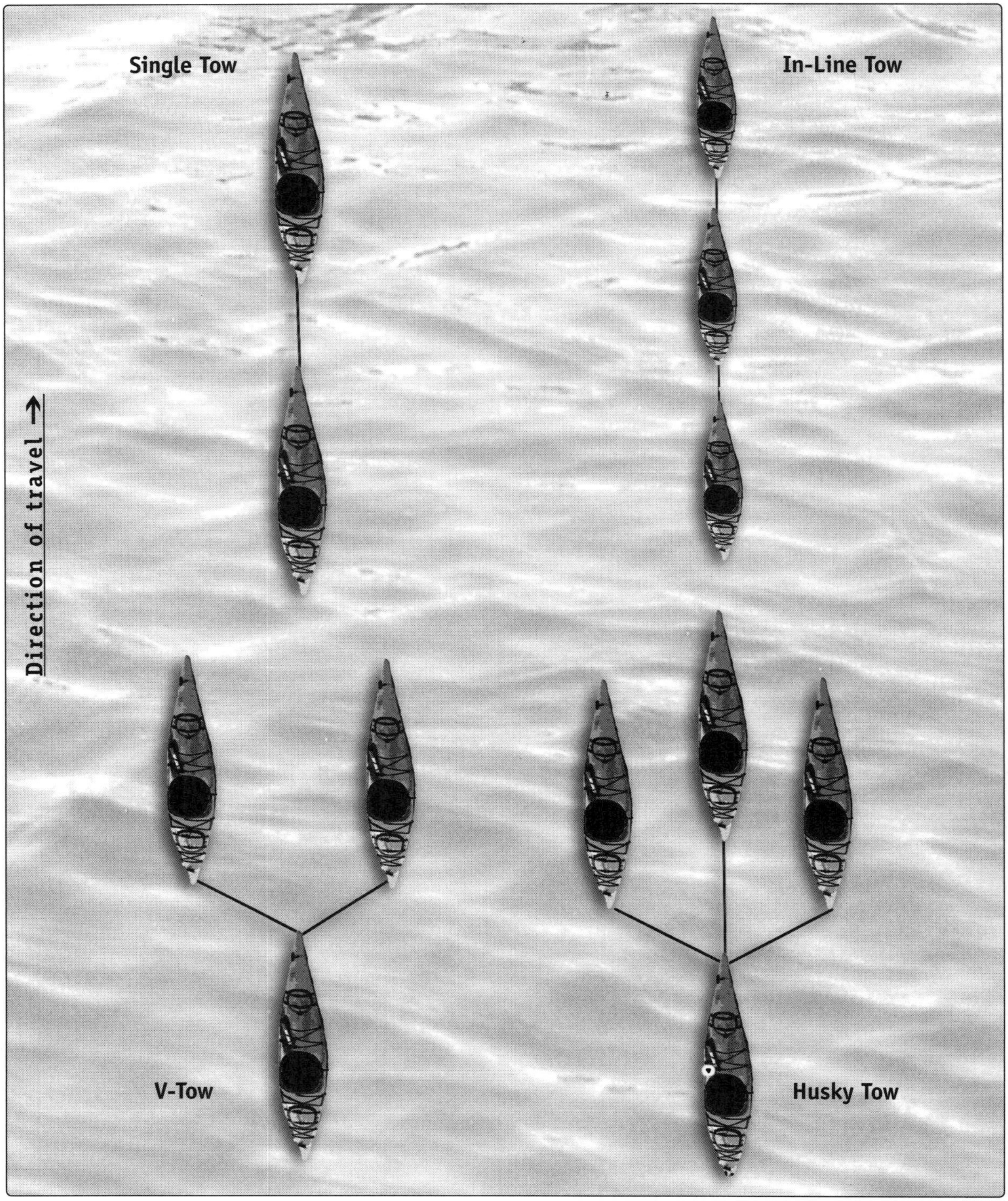

Single Tow
In-Line Tow
Direction of travel →
V-Tow
Husky Tow

Husky Tow

Basically a combination of a Single Tow with two "wing" paddlers using a V-Tow, this person three-person configuration is like a team of huskies, fast and powerful. Also like a sled team, it is not always easy to keep the dogs from clashing. In rough conditions especially, the Husky Tow requires fine teamwork and boat control to keep the complex affair from ending up in a tangle of paddlers, boats, and rope.

Towing Incapacitated Paddlers

Special tows are called for when a paddler can't stay upright or paddle by himself due to injury, illness, or some other reason. You won't be able to tow someone who keeps tipping upside down. It's possible to use a Contact Tow (described earlier) to move a paddler who can barely stay upright in a kayak. But there are two more efficient methods: the Rafted Tow and the Paddlefloat-Supported Tow.

Rafted Tow

We have used this technique to tow unstable paddlers in rough water after a capsize and for sea-sick paddlers. The stabilizing paddler grabs on to the back of the cockpit coaming of the incapacitated paddler, who then leans over onto the stabilizer's front deck.

Here are some tips for Rafted Tows. Use one of the smaller people in the group to stabilize, if possible: There is no sense towing any more weight than you have to. On longer tows you may need to change stabilizers to give their hands a rest. To simplify the change, be sure to hook the tow line onto the bow of the paddler being towed, not the one doing the stabilizing. Otherwise you'll have to change the tow line each time you want to change stabilizers. Since it is difficult for one person to tow a raft of two paddlers, this may be a good time to use an In-Line Tow or other team-towing technique if you have several paddlers with tow ropes handy.

Paddlefloat-Supported Tow

We refer to this method as the "Buck Tow" for the instructor friend who told us about it. Instead of another person, this technique uses a paddlefloat on one or both blades to stabilize an unsteady paddler. It might not work with a sick or injured paddler, but Buck used it successfully to stabilize a paddler after repeated capsizes in rough

Rafted Tow:
One rescuer tows while another grabs onto the cockpit coaming of the unstable or incapacitated paddler to stabilize him.

Paddlefloat-Supported Tow:
This tow employs two paddlefloats to stabilize the towee.

seas. It worked only because the paddler had enough control to hold himself upright using a paddlefloat while being towed. A less able paddler might be able to slump down in his seat to lower his center of gravity and wedge the paddle under his arms. The Buck Tow's advantages over a Rafted Tow are that it's less work, since you're only towing one paddler, and that you can use it if you don't have a third paddler in your group for stabilization. One drawback is that if you put a paddlefloat on both blades, someone in the group will no longer have direct access to her own paddlefloat if she should capsize.

Towing Safety

Use caution whenever you're towing—it's a risky business. Use quick-release mechanisms and keep a PFD knife or trauma scissors handy. Anytime you add long pieces of rope to a paddling situation, you also add the chance that gear and people will become tangled in them, especially if someone

capsizes during towing and you have to do a rescue. Another risk involves being speared in the ribs by the boat you are towing if you use a line that is too short (see the line length recommendations below). Still, these risks seem more than justified when you think of the possible consequences of not having a tow line when you really need one.

Gear for Towing

Towing gear ranges from a simple length of rope (not recommended) to elaborate systems employing carabiners for quickly attaching to towed boats, shock-absorbing bungees to cushion the effects of yanking, and quick-release features allowing you to unhitch quickly in an emergency or capsize. Such features drive up the cost of towing systems, so you need to consider which ones you really need and how much you're willing to pay for them. Whatever the system, it needs to work for *you* (which implies that you'll need some practice to familiarize yourself with your equipment). Keep the following features in mind before laying down the bucks for the towing system that will meet your needs.

Accessibility: It's nice if your system can be quickly and efficiently deployed, especially if you might have to use it in rough water. It's also convenient if it repacks easily after towing. Ideally all metal parts, such as carabiners, zippers, and hooks, should be made of stainless steel or anodized aluminum so they don't corrode and become jammed.

Shock Absorption: A bungee integrated into the tow rope can soften the tugging action. While some towers find this "tow jerk" uncomfortable (especially in systems that attach to the body via waist belts or PFDs), others don't seem to mind. Personally, we don't find towing to be all that uncomfortable without a bungee, especially if we're using inherently stretchy line.

Versatility: The ability to easily trade towing systems (and towing duties) among paddling partners is a nice option. It saves time if the person towing can quickly hand off the line already in use without having to rig a new line or repack the old. We've found that sharing is easier with a tow belt (assuming the waist belt can be easily adjusted) than with a boat-specific deck-bag or PFD system.

Visibility: Brightly colored floating line is easier to see and handle than dark line that has sunk below the surface.

Length: While 15 feet is about the shortest length that will work well on flat water, in rougher conditions we recommend about twice that length to avoid being speared. Once Roger was towing a student in following seas. He descended into a trough between swells and heard a shout from behind: *"Lookout!"* His too-short tow rope had pulled the student down the face of the following swell, causing her boat to surf—right across his back deck, her bow missing his kidneys by inches. Since then we've found that keeping 25 to 30 feet between you

and the boat being towed has worked well. Longer than that is more line than we want to bother with repacking.

Strength: Most ¼-inch kernmantle line will be plenty strong for towing purposes. Larger diameters are unnecessarily bulky, while thinner lines may push the breaking point and be harder to handle.

Pieces of Rope and Tow Bags

Although not exactly quick and convenient, a simple length of rope will work in a pinch, and you can't beat the price. The towing "system" we first used when working for an outfitter in the San Juans was no more than a 15-foot length of ⅜-inch nylon line rigged with a cheap plastic hook on one end—total cost less than five bucks, including hook. The guides kept them under the front-deck bungees. For towing, we'd attach the hook to our rear-deck bungee, tie a bowline to the bow toggle of the towee's boat, and start paddling. Better than nothing, this simple system was slow and awkward to deploy, difficult to release quickly in an emergency, and put more strain on the bungees than they were designed for.

For a higher-tech version of the piece-of-rope system, there are various commercial tow bags on the market, basically consisting of a length of rope stowed in a convenient drawstring pouch. What you're paying for besides convenient packaging is typically strong, brightly colored line that floats. But be aware that you'll still need some way to attach a tow bag to you or your kayak. Be careful about buying the common tow bags designed for whitewater kayaking. There are some important differences.

For example, the 8- to 10-foot tow lines often used in whitewater towing systems barely clear the back deck of longer sea kayaks. Conversely, the 50-plus feet of heavyweight line found in most river throw bags is overkill for towing sea kayaks: All that length gives you plenty of extra rope to tangle into unintentional macramé during use and takes that much longer to repack; the length, along with the heavy

⅝-inch diameter, also makes for a bulky bag to stow on your deck.

Another consideration with ropes and bags is deciding where to attach them. Since it's more efficient to tow from the center of the boat, some people tie off around their cockpit or rig an attachment point behind their cockpit. An instructor friend of ours mounted a cam cleat from a sailing hardware store on her back deck, where a flick of her wrist quickly releases it in an emergency.

Tow Belts

Considering accessibility, ease of sharing with others, and cost, we prefer the elegant simplicity of a waist-belt towing system. Commercial tow belts tend to be sturdy and sleek on the hip. Typically the line is stored in a bag that is sewn to a webbing belt held tight by a rugged, quick-release cam buckle like an old-fashioned seat belt. Unfortunately, some seem to have a small, sideways-facing openings that make repacking at sea somewhat awkward, especially in rough conditions.

Our preference is for top-loading styles with plenty of room for your hand, so we have gone to making our own. We've had fairly good luck buying inexpensive fanny packs from a sporting goods store, tying 30 feet of ¼-inch nylon line around the belt, and stowing it in the pouch. The weak link in these homemade jobs is either the wimpy ½-inch plastic buckle on the fanny pack or the single stitching where the webbing belt is sewn into each end of the bag. Although the system seems to hold up in most situations, towing loaded kayaks in rough seas can rip the belt off the bag. We now sew our own beefier versions, using bags (with corrosion-resistant nylon zippers) attached to a single length of 1-inch webbing that encircles the waist.

Deck Bags

If you find tow belts uncomfortable (an instructor friend of ours says the pull hurts her bad back), or if the idea of a having a tow line wrapped around your body in rough water makes you nervous, then maybe a deck-bag towing system is for you. These systems are also good for people who enjoy customizing their boats. Generally you'll have to drill holes to mount a quick-release cam cleat. If you want to be extra sure that your new deck hardware doesn't pull out, add a layer of fiberglass to the deck first.

Still, unless you have a problem with waist belts—such as a bad back or an understandable dislike for having ropes lashed around your middle—we don't see any advantages to deck bags.

Rescue Vests

These nifty, high-tech designs basically marry a tow belt with a PFD. They're the most expensive tow systems around, but not that pricey when you consider that you're getting both a tow belt and a PFD. Line is stowed handily in a front pocket of the PFD or in a small bag attached to a quick-release webbing belt worn around the chest. Since it rides higher than a waist belt, it has the advantage of being less likely to tangle in the rear-deck rigging or rudder during use. But this does little to speak to the bad-back or don't-like-line-wrapped-around-my-body concerns of deck-bag advocates. Besides cost, there is one other potential drawback: Unlike a simple tow belt, the integrated system is not as easy to swap among paddling partners on the water.

Short Lines and Cow Tails

In addition to our 30-foot tow lines, we both also use some form of short line. We find these 3- to 8-foot lines especially convenient for retrieving drifting boats or for quick, short-distance towing. We've used them, for instance, to tow a boat away from rocks or surf, especially during a rescue when we didn't want to hassle with deploying and then having to stow our full-length lines. Roger uses a commercially made cow tail (a 3-foot length of webbing with a bungee inside and a carabiner attached to one end; it's designed for towing white-water kayaks) attached to a rescue vest. Jan uses an 8-foot length of line that stows in a separate pocket of her tow belt. Short lines are quick, but their use is limited, and you must be careful not to get speared by the bow of the towed kayak when using them.

Considering our own towing needs—quick, easy access; ability to share the towing system easily (so we can also share the towing duties); and reasonable cost—we're biased toward tow belts, and we feel naked leaving shore without them. But you may have your own needs (and a more generous budget). Whatever system you use, there's no reason not to paddle with *something*, if only a length of rope. After all, the lunch you save may be your own.

■ Retrieving Boats and Swimmers

"Remember, *always hang on to your boat*" is one of the most important reminders we give our students during rescue practice. The only thing worse than being up the creek without a paddle, we have learned the hard way, is to be out in open seas without a boat. In calm water with no wind, you can get away with floating leisurely beside your boat, pieces of gear bobbing around you like so many apples in a barrel. However, we strongly encourage you to get in the habit of hanging on to your gear and using solid, rough-water rescue techniques even while practicing in flat water. We have seen people who regularly practice rescues in swimming pools make the mistake of letting their paddles or kayaks drift away unnoticed while performing rescues on the sea. Letting go of a kayak during a real-life rescue is a serious breech of safety etiquette that can endanger the rescuer as well as the swimmer. In even a light breeze, a boat can quickly blow away from you faster than you can swim. We first wrote about this topic in *Sea Kayaker* at the editor's request following near fatality in Puget Sound where one of two kayakers capsized and let go of his kayak in a storm.

Still, sometimes the worst happens, and you're faced with reuniting a swimmer and his kayak. In a nutshell, there are two main ways to do this: You can either bring the kayak to the swimmer or the swimmer to the kayak. Generally it's much easier to move an empty kayak than to drag a soggy swimmer.

So although general safety guidelines would suggest that you "Always rescue people before gear," in some cases the "Keep it simple" guideline suggests the opposite. However, if there's the slightest chance you could lose track of the swimmer in rough seas, you'll need to go after the swimmer first, as described in Retrieving Swimmers, below. Otherwise there's not much point to retrieving a kayak if there's nobody to put in it.

Boat Retrieval Techniques

Ideally one rescuer keeps track of the swimmer while the other retrieves the boat, but if you are alone, you can still go for the kayak first, provided there is no danger of losing sight of the swimmer. To do this you can use your bow to push the kayak (*bulldozing*), grab the kayak and push it toward the swimmer (*herding*), or use a rope to tow the kayak (*towing*).

Bulldozing

The simplest way to retrieve a drifting boat is to "bulldoze" it, using the bow of your own kayak to push it back to the swimmer. Drifting kayaks tend to turn beam-on to the seas (perpendicular to the wind). The most efficient technique is to paddle to the downwind side, balance your bow amidships, and T-bone the kayak while shoving it toward the swimmer. It is not easy to move a boat quickly in this manner, but you will be stopping its drift, giving the swimmer a chance to stroke toward a nonmoving target.

Herding

In choppy conditions it can be difficult to keep your bow in contact with the loose boat, so bulldozing may not be an option. Before you pull out your tow rope (or if you don't have this essential piece of safety gear), you might try herding the drifting kayak—paddling up alongside it, grabbing it, and pushing it ahead of you repeatedly in the direction you want it to go. This awkward technique is good only for short distances.

Bulldozing a kayak involves pushing it back to the swimmer who has lost it.

Short-Line Towing

If the simpler techniques of bulldozing and herding aren't working, bring the boat to the paddler by towing it. (For more on towing techniques, see the preceding section.) We used to carry only our standard 30-foot tow lines, but now, in addition to this long line, we also carry short lines (3 to 8 feet). These are much quicker to deploy and repack and seem to work well for towing gear short distances upwind. (Towing a kayak downwind in following seas with a short line, you run the risk of being speared in the kidneys; usually, however, you'll be towing upwind when returning a boat to a swimmer, so this won't be an issue.) Short lines also have another advantage: There is less line in the water for the swimmer to get tangled in.

A capsized kayak is harder to tow than a righted one, so it's often worth the time and effort to right it and drain it (with a T Rescue) before towing it. (The exceptions are towing only a few feet, and towing in rough seas where you think the boat may capsize again.) Although this might seem to take longer, the time you spend emptying the boat may well be made up in faster towing and rescue time once you reach the swimmer.

Six-Pack Rule: Whatever method you use to return the boat, it is within your rights as a rescuer to remind the swimmer—typically *before* returning the boat and completing the reentry—of the "Six-Pack Rule." Section IV, paragraph 2, of this rule clearly states that "any paddler who lets go of his or her gear during a rescue owes a six-pack of B.O.C. [beverage of choice] to whomever shall retrieve that gear."

Short-Line Towing is a way to quickly return a kayak to its swimmer.

REAL LIFE RESCUES

Practice Makes Perfect

The first time we taught a rough-water rescue class, we practiced in calm water before paddling out of Moss Landing Harbor onto Monterey Bay one typically windy summer afternoon. Seas were running 4 to 6 feet, with the usual 15- to 20-knot northwesterlies kicking up whitecaps all around. During a T Rescue, one of the students in the water had her hands slip off her kayak after she'd pushed the stern down to help the rescue boat lift the bow. Just then a wind wave washed the boat an arm's length away.

She lunged for it as a second wave washed it several feet farther. She immediately started swimming after her boat, but the next swell surfed her kayak, still held bow-up by her surprised rescuer, a boat length away. Within a few seconds—about the time it took for her to swim the half-dozen strokes to cover the boat length of distance her kayak had been from her—her kayak and rescuer were three more boat lengths away and gaining momentum in the wind and chop. The swimmer, however, beginning to see the futility of racing the wind, was beginning to tire.

The rescuer was dazed at first, not knowing what to do. As the gap widened, she first tried shouting at the swimmer to swim harder. Yeah, right. Then she tried putting the boat back in the water and bulldozing it. Impossible in the chop. By now the swimmer was nearly 100 yards away, bobbing and disappearing occasionally behind the swells. The drifting kayak was heading for shore, over ½ mile away, where large dumping waves pounded the beach. It looked like our swimmer was in for a long, rough swim, and suddenly our practice session had turned quite real. It was about time, it seemed, for the instructors to jump in and save the day.

But the dose of reality seemed to spur the class into action. Before we had time to take over, two students headed for the swimmer, rafted up, and got her to climb out of the cold water onto their back decks. In the meantime a third student clipped her new tow line onto the drifting kayak and began towing it back to its owner. As quickly as the situation had gotten out of hand, it was back in control again. Within a minute or two the swimmer was back in her boat and everyone was a bit wiser. Using techniques learned in practice, they had managed to orchestrate a perfect, real-life rescue.

Roger + Jan

Retrieving Swimmers

In rough seas where losing sight of the swimmer is a possibility, forget the boat. Remember: People take priority over gear. As always, approach swimmers cautiously, making sure they are not going to scramble onto your boat in a panic and capsize you. Ideally you have a partner who is retrieving the kayak, because the likelihood of catching a windblown kayak once you have a swimmer in tow is poor: Humans are about as hydrodynamically streamlined as a bag of bricks, and towing one through the water is about as easy. You have a few quick options for short distances, none of them very efficient. You can tow swimmers from your rear toggle, have them grab on to your bow and try to bulldoze them, have them climb onto your back deck, or tow them with a tow rope.

Toggle Tow

Quick and easy, the toggle tow is a good option over short distances, but it can be extremely tiring. To lessen the drag of towing an errant swimmer, don't be shy about asking him to help out as much as possible. After he grabs your stern toggle, get him to raise his legs to streamline his body as much as possible. Then it is acceptable to shout at him to "kick *hard*, like the scurvy dog you are for letting go of your boat!" Don't forget to look back often. Roger once had a swimmer let go in the middle of a tow. He was paddling so hard he didn't realize it at first and went several boat lengths before he realized she was no longer holding on and had not bothered to utter a peep to let him know.

Bulldozing a Swimmer

If you are afraid the swimmer might let go or you just want to keep your eye on him, you might try having him wrap his arms and legs around your bow while you bulldoze him through the water on his back. Most people, however, will find this technique less efficient than toggle towing.

PFD Tow

In a worst-case scenario you could retrieve a swimmer who is too weak or hypothermic to hang on (or unconscious) by clipping your tow rope to his PFD and towing him to land. By running your line through both shoulder straps, instead of just one, an unconscious swimmer will run a better chance of staying face-up during the tow. Also, never give up: Resuscitation of cold-water drowning victims has been successful after amazing lengths of time. Because of the so-called mammalian diving response, respiration and heart rate can slow dramatically in cold water; some victims have been resuscitated without brain damage after an hour or more.

Back-Deck Swimmer Rescue

To cover any distance, you'll make much better progress, as well as minimize the effects of immersion in cold water, if you can transport the swimmer on your back deck—assuming, of course, that he doesn't capsize you in the process. (Paddling with an extra person aboard is a challenging technique requiring good balance and bracing skills, and we definitely recommend practicing ahead of time in shallow water.) The swimmer

Bulldozing a swimmer is one way of returning a swimmer to his boat.

In the Back-Deck Swimmer Rescue,
the swimmer rides the stern, keeping his weight low and as close to the paddler as possible.

needs to board carefully, staying low on his belly and getting as close to the rescuer as possible to help maintain balance and boat trim. If the swimmer didn't let go of his paddle along with his boat, the extra paddle may get in the way—his tendency will be to hold it perpendicularly across the back deck in front of his face, where it will hinder the end of your stroke when you try to paddle. Have him stow the paddle beneath him parallel to the kayak. If you are unlikely to retrieve the loose boat and the situation looks ugly, just toss the worthless piece of junk overboard (the spare paddle, that is, not the swimmer). To make faster progress, the swimmer can try to reduce the drag of his legs and feet by lifting them partway out of the water. If it's not too unstable, you might even have him assist you by paddling the kayak with his hands as if it were a big surfboard.

Besides balance, steering control will also be a challenge with all that extra weight on your stern, especially in wind. If you are having trouble staying on course, try using your rudder (if you

have one). You might also try raising it if it's already down, since the swimmer's weight on the rudder might act as a pivot point for the wind to blow your bow farther off course. As a last resort your passenger can try sliding his legs back into the water on one side, carefully so as not to cause a capsize, and kicking his feet to shove the stern around until you're heading in the right direction again. But you may need to use this dicey maneuver repeatedly to stay on course. If there is an extra paddler, you can have her hook a tow line to your bow, which will greatly enhance speed and steering.

There are a lot of options for reuniting swimmers with their boats, but none of them is particularly efficient. The best option is to paddle with buddies who always hang on to their gear after capsize so you'll never have to resort to these techniques in real life. Still, it is a good idea to practice just in case you find yourself in the bad company of someone who has gotten himself up a creek without a kayak.

Chapter 9

Old–School Rescues & Inflatable Safety Devices

- ## HI Rescue
- ## All In Rescue
- ## Inflatable Devices

The techniques and devices described in this chapter are those we've experimented with but subsequently cast aside in favor of alternatives that we think accomplish the same objectives more quickly and effectively. We recognize, however, that one person's refuse may be another person's treasure, so we encourage you to play around with these and add them to your repertoire as you see fit.

HI Rescue

The HI, also referred to as the Ipswich Rescue, is an old-school assisted rescue in which two paddlers team up to rescue a third paddler/swimmer after a capsize. Once popular in Britain, its use has been superseded for the most part by the T Rescue, especially among North American paddlers. Like the T, this reentry takes its name from the configuration of the kayaks. The two paddlers involved in the rescue set up parallel to each other with their paddles making a bridge between them, forming an H.

The swimmer's kayak is dragged between them, and the bow of his boat is lifted onto the paddle bridge. When the cockpit of the swimmer's kayak reaches the paddles, it is seesawed to drain the water. As you might imagine, dragging a swamped kayak across the paddle shafts could damage all but the sturdiest paddles, especially if the kayak has no bulkheads and needs to be teeter-tottered across the paddles with water in its stern. Once the boat is drained, it is stabilized between the two rescue boats. The swimmer reenters his cockpit by climbing up from between the kayaks, either onto his back deck as in the finish of a T Rescue or feet-first between two of the kayaks, as in the British Style or Between Boats Reentry.

While many paddlers have been able to make this rescue work successfully over the years, it has several drawbacks, in our minds, compared to the T. Besides risking damage to the paddles used in the bridge, the HI cannot be done by a single rescuer. A certain degree of coordination between the two rescuers is also implied, which may not be much of a problem for skilled paddlers but could cause fits for others, especially in rough seas. The HI was common in the days when bulkheads were not. The idea was probably that it was better to risk damaging the paddles than to do a TX Rescue and risk damage to the decks of two fiberglass kayaks by teeter-tottering the swamped boat over the rescue boat. If you are worried about deck damage from doing a TX on fiberglass kayaks without bulkheads, we recommend either a simple Reenter and Pump Rescue or else carrying very sturdy paddles. Otherwise, we can't really think of any situation where an HI would be a more efficient style of assisted reentry than a T. Those interested in antiques, however, might like adding this curiosity to their rescue repertoire.

■ All In Rescue

The All In Rescue is another old-school British import not practiced much nowadays. The name *All In* refers to a situation in which a sudden wave or squall capsizes every paddler in a group—they are *all in* the water. The technique preceded common usage of the Paddlefloat Self-Rescue, so it was assumed that all the swimmers were incapable of rescuing themselves. What to do? The idea is that the swimmers swim their kayaks together to keep the group united while they help each other back into their boats. The rescue starts with one swimmer dragging his inverted kayak over the upturned hull of a second kayak to drain the water out of the cockpit. In the meantime the other swimmers do very little besides bob about like ice cubes in a gin and tonic.

Once the first boat is drained, it is turned upright and placed parallel to the second kayak. Swimmer number two reaches across his over-turned hull to stabilize the righted kayak by holding on to its cockpit coaming. A paddle is held across the two kayaks for added stability, while the first swimmer pulls herself up onto her back deck, as in other assisted rescues. This first person reenters her cockpit and replaces her sprayskirt. With one paddler back in her boat, she can then rescue the second paddler with one of the assisted rescues, such as the T, TX, or Reenter and Pump. As more swimmers are assisted back into their kayaks, a domino effect of assisted reentries ensues until all in the group are back in their kayaks. A quicker option might be for the swimmers of a larger group to pair up to get several reentries started at the same time.

This rescue requires a fair amount of synchronized swimming effort, since the kayaks first need to be moved to each other—no small feat for swimmers who are encumbered by wearing paddling gear and dragging their kayaks and paddles. An All In Rescue would be most applicable in a situation where at least two paddlers capsize in fairly close proximity to one another—for example, one paddler capsizes while in the process of T Rescuing his partner. Another problem is the time it takes to recover all the swimmers. Those not involved in the first reentry or two will end up floating for several minutes, getting colder and colder, waiting their turn to be rescued. This is why we strongly encourage all paddlers in a group to be self-sufficient by carrying a paddlefloat and the skills to use it.

■ Inflatable Devices: Back Up, Sponsons, and Sea–Seat

The original Eskimo paddlers sometimes carried sealskin hunting floats on their decks. Attached to a harpoon line, these beachball-sized floats were used primarily to prevent a speared animal from sinking. After a capsize, however, a paddler could also grab the float from under the deck rigging and use it instead of his paddle to roll himself back upright. Although sealskin is no longer in vogue, modern recreational paddlers have a number of inflatable safety devices to choose from in addition to the trusty paddlefloat described earlier.

Our inclusion of these devices here is not intended as an endorsement but only to inform you of some options. It is interesting to note that none of them has gained the widespread acceptance of the paddlefloat, and as far as we know only one of the devices has more than one manufacturer. Our philosophy is to beware of gear-intensive techniques. It has been our experience that the overwhelming majority of our students are able to master many of the recovery techniques we have presented in this book fairly quickly when given good instruction and a little time to practice. We have also found that gear tends to fail in ways that well-practiced skills do not. That said, we also believe that paddlers will be safer by expanding their options.

Depending on their ability—or inability—to perform the other recoveries in this book, some paddlers may find these devices to be useful fall-back gear that increases their margin of safety. Other paddlers might find them absolutely essential for survival, while still others will consider them so much unnecessary flotsam. As with all the rescue skills, the only way to find out what works for you is to practice.

Back Up Self–Rescue Float

The Back Up is a high-tech version of the hunting floats originally used by Eskimo paddlers. It is stored, deflated, on deck in a sleek plastic canister about the size of a tall can of beer. Basically it functions as an "instant Bow Rescue in a can." After a capsize you simply reach up, and instead of pulling on the grab loop of your sprayskirt for a wet exit, you yank on the handle protruding from the Back Up canister. Attached to the handle is a float that quickly self-inflates with a CO_2 cartridge. You use the float to roll back upright without leaving your cockpit.

This nifty device is probably less useful for novice paddlers than for those with more experience, especially with Bow Rescues. It requires

The Back Up Self-Rescue Float is an "instant Bow Rescue in a can."

that you can keep a cool head after capsize, that you have the hip snap skills to right yourself, and that you have a sprayskirt that will stay on your coaming. Assuming these are all true, a Back Up could provide a handy option for staying in your kayak after a capsize. If you do end up in the water, the manufacturer claims that you can also use the Back Up in place of a paddlefloat. While this might be *possible*, we didn't think that the attachment points are very secure, especially for use in rough water. So we recommend carrying a separate paddlefloat and canning the dual-purpose idea.

Sponsons

Sponsons are essentially inflatable pontoons that attach to either side of your kayak much like the training wheels on your first bicycle. And like training wheels, they provide extra stability but also hinder performance somewhat. But then, nothing hinders performance quite like a capsize.

For sponsons to work properly, it is recommended that they be rigged and adjusted for your

Sponsors, inflatable pontoons that attach to either side of your kayak, offer a stable rescue platform.

specific kayak prior to paddling. The 40-inch-long inflatable tubes are designed to be attached at water level along either side of your cockpit. With any luck you can simply tie the Fastex buckles into existing deck rigging on your bow and on the back deck just behind the seat, and then clip the sponsons into place when you need them. Otherwise you'll need to add attachment points with the appropriate spacing.

After a capsize the idea is that you will simply pull out the sponsons, snap them into their prefitted buckles, and inflate them to create a stable rescue platform. Once they are in place, the sponsons' main advantage over a paddlefloat is that they continue to offer support after reentry even while you're paddling the swamped kayak. They can also be deployed from the cockpit in rough seas to prevent a capsize in the first place, be used to tow an injured paddler, or simply create a more stable platform for photography or

fishing. Sponsons will cause some drag and slow your progress, the manufacturer claims, by approximately 20 percent. We find this a reasonable estimate.

In addition to this small loss of performance, sponsons generally take at least twice as long to inflate as a paddlefloat, since you have to blow up and rig two chambers instead of only one. This extra rigging time is what we consider the main disadvantage of sponsons, especially for those who don't really require the additional stability (that is, those paddlers who have learned that with good technique, a Paddlefloat Self-Rescue is a perfectly viable rough-water reentry). If you do require extra stability or are simply seeking belt-and-suspenders redundancy, adding sponsons to your selection of safety gear may be well worth it. We would like to note, however, that one rather portly student who was able to reenter her kayak using a paddlefloat and a sling was not able to do so with sponsons: Even with the sponsons in place and fully inflated, she was heavy enough to pull the boat over on top of herself while trying to climb in.

Sea–Seat

The manufacturer describes the Sea-Seat as a personal life raft. Envision a square inner tube 3 feet across with no hole in the middle and you'll get a pretty good picture of this device. Instead of a hole, the Sea-Seat has a depression for your rear, which will keep it out of the cold water. It takes some practice to learn how to climb onto without capsizing the device itself, but it is fairly stable once you are ensconced firmly, and all but your feet will be kept out of the cold water.

From the seat, you can either slide sideways into your cockpit or, if you've lost your kayak entirely, paddle the "raft" itself. Since it has no CO_2 cartridges, this device takes several minutes to inflate by mouth. But it might be the next best thing to carrying a spare kayak or to towing a regular life raft along behind you.

If you feel that you'd like to experiment with some inflatable backup options to your paddle-float, we've included the contact information for the devices described above. (Back–up self-rescue float, 604–224–4010; Sea Wings sponsons, 705–549–3722; Thermofloat Sea-Seat, 250–382–1243.) But no matter how many of these backups you add to your rescue gear, you'll need to get comfortable with them first in flat water and then in the type of conditions you're likely to need them in if you expect them to work in an emergency. All the inflatable toys in the world won't save you if you don't know how to use them.

Have fun practicing!

Index

All In Rescue, 120
Assisted T Rescue, *see* Rafted T Rescue

bail out plans, 10
bilge pumps, 13–14
Boat Over Boat Rescue, *see* TX Rescue
Bow Lift Fancy Flip, 42–44
    with Scramble Rescue, 64
    Real Life Rescue, 67
Bow Rescue, *see* Eskimo Bow Rescue
Bracing, 19–28
    Low Brace, 21–24
    High Brace, 21, 24–25
    Running Low Brace, 25
    Low Brace Turn, 26
    Sweep Brace, 26
    Sculling Brace, 26–27
    Greenland Sculling, 27
    Bracing practice drills, 27–28
    Hyper Brace, 27
British Style Reentry, 58–59

Cleopatra's Needle, 89–91
common hazards, 2–4
Cowboy Rescue, *see* Scramble
C to C, 21;
    C to C Roll, 76–77

double kayak rescues, 92–98

Eskimo Bow Rescue, 68–73
    practice tips, 70–73
    Real Life Bow Rescue, 72
Eskimo Roll, 27, 73–77
    Sweep Roll, 74–76
    C to C Roll, 76–77
    in loaded kayak, 92
    in double kayak, 96

float plans, 17
freeboard, 92

Hand of God, 88
Head Dink, 21
HI Rescue, 119–20
Hip Flick, *see* Hip Snap
Hip Snap, 20–23, 70–71
hypothermia, 4–5

incapacitated paddler, *see* Scoop Rescue,
    Hand of God
inflatable rescue devices, 120–23
    see also paddlefloat

J-Lean, 20–23

L

loaded boat rescues, 92
  Real Life Rescue, 94

P

Paddlefloat Self Rescue, 13, 35–42
  practice tips, 44–45
  Real Life Rescues, 44
  Paddlefloat Reenter and Roll, 64–66
  use of paddlefloat device for Eskimo Roll
    practice, 77
  Paddlefloat with Sling, 80–82
  with double kayaks, 93–95
panicking swimmers, dealing with, 45, 87
PFD (personal flotation devices), 12
practicing rescues, 8–10, 20–33
  rough water practice, 32–33, 98–101
  Paddlefloat Rescue practice tips, 44–45
  T-Rescue practice tips, 49–52
  Scramble practice tips, 64
  Bow Rescue, 70–71
  Real Life practice, 67, 116

R

Rafted T Rescue, 54–55
  Real Life Rescue, 57
rand, 29
recovery, 1–2
Reenter and Pump, 55–56
Reenter and Roll, 64–68
reentry, 1–2
rock garden rescues, 100–101
rough water rescues and reentries, 32–33, 98–101

S

safety gear, 7, 11–17
safety guidelines, 4–10
Scoop Rescue, 86–87

Scramble Rescue, 61–64
  "Taco" version, 64
  practice tips, 64
  Real Life Scramble, 67
  with double kayak, 95–96
Side By Side Rescue, *see* Reenter and Pump
Signaling devices, 15–17
  whistles and air horns, 15
  flares, 15
  radios and cell phones, 15–16
sinking kayaks, *see* Cleopatra's Needle
sit-on-top kayak rescues, 98
Sling Rescue, 14, 79–86
  Paddlefloat with Sling, 80–82
  T Rescue with Sling, 82–86
  Real Life Sling Rescue, 85
Stirrup Rescue, *see* Sling Rescue
stirrup, *see* Sling Rescue
surf zone rescues, 98–100
swimmer rescues, 114–17

T

T Rescue, 45–54
  "pit-to-pit" stabilization technique, 48
  practice tips, 49–52
  Real Life T Rescues, 50–51, 57, 85, 94, 116
  with sling, 82–86
  on loaded kayaks, 92
  on double kayaks, 96–97
tired paddlers, *see* Sling Rescues
towing, 103–18
  Swim-Tow, 100
  Contact Tow, 107–08
  towing safety, 111
  gear for towing, 111–14
  Toggle-Tow, 101, 116–17
  Real Life Rescues, 94, 116
TX Rescue, 52–53

W

weather checks, 5–7
Wet Exit, 29–30

About the Authors

Roger Schumann and Jan Shriner share a love for aquatic environments, from the fragile web of the upland watersheds to the wild energy of the California coast they call home. They combined forces after meeting in the San Juan Islands of Washington, creating Eskape Sea Kayaking of Santa Cruz, a small instructional sea kayaking business through which they continue to run trips from the San Juans to the Sea of Cortez. Both Jan and Roger are nationally certified sea kayaking instructors and instructor trainers and have been selected by the American Canoe Assocation (ACA) to work on its national committee to develop the Coastal Kayaking curriculum. In addition, Jan and Roger are co-authors of *The Guide to Sea Kayaking Central and Northern California*, winner of the 2000 National Outdoor Book Award in the Adventure Guidebook Category, and co-editors of *The Basic Essentials of Sea Kayaking*, both published by The Globe Pequot Press. They are also frequent contributors to *Sea Kayaker* magazine.